# GREAT
# KNITS
## *for*
# KIDS

# Debbie Bliss

# GREAT KNITS

## *for*

# KIDS

Trafalgar Square Publishing

*For my mother, Mid*

First published in the United States of America in 1997 by
Trafalgar Square Publishing, North Pomfret, Vermont 05053

**Printed and bound in Spain by Book Print**

First published in Great Britain in 1997
by Collins & Brown Limited, London

1 3 5 7 9 8 6 4 2

Library of Congress Catalog Card Number: 96-60984

ISBN 1-57076-076-4

Conceived, edited and designed by Collins & Brown Limited

Designer: Carole Perks

Photography: Sandra Lousada

Reproduction by HBM Print Ltd

# Contents

# Introduction

*Great Knits for Kids* is my latest collection of hand-knits for children, and for the first time the designs cover the age range from babies right up to children aged ten. I have loved having the opportunity to create designs for seven to ten-year-olds as exciting, wearable styles for older children can be hard to find.

There are 27 designs to choose from: fisher knits that use traditional stitches in subtly-faded denim yarn, delicate cotton cardigans, classic country house tweeds and a versatile wrap that can double up as a cot cover or a throw.

There is something to suit all knitting abilities, with basic stocking stitch and garter stitch for beginners, texture with cables and bobbles for Aran lovers and both simple and more intricate Fair Isles for knitters who like to work with colour patterning.

As always, depending on the style, I have given some of the designs generous size allowances as I think that children are used to wearing casual clothes and should feel comfortable and unrestricted when wearing knitwear. However, as all the patterns quote actual measurements, you can knit up whichever size you prefer.

Debbie Bliss

# Tunic Top with Bobble Detail
page 43
# Cable and Bobble Tunic page 44

## Cabled, Zipped Jacket with Collar
page 45

## Ribbed Denim
### Sweater page 47

# Stocking-stitch Sweater with Collar
page 53

## Lace-edged Cardigan page 54

## Floral Cardigan page 56

# Moss-stitch Tunic with Hat
page 58

# Guernsey with Ribbed Yoke
page 59

# Denim Wrap page 60
# Moss-stitch Beret page 61

**Cabled Tunic with Shawl Collar** page 68

**Shawl-collared Jacket with Fair Isle Bands** page 69

**Garter-stitch Jacket**
page 72

**Tweed Jacket
with Cable
Beret** page 76

*previous page*
**Ribbed Sweater with Stripes** page 52
*this page*
**Black and White Fair Isle Cardigan** page 78

**Simple Striped Sweater** page 79

# Basic Information

## NOTES

Figures for larger sizes are are given in ( ) brackets. Where only one figure appears, this applies to all sizes.

Work figures given in [ ] brackets the number of times stated afterwards. Alternatively, they give the resultant number of stitches.

Where 0 appears, no stitches or rows are worked for this size.

The yarn amounts given in the instructions are based on average requirements and should therefore be considered approximate. If you want to use a substitute yarn, choose a yarn of the same type and weight as the one recommended. The following descriptions of the various Rowan yarns are meant as a guide to the yarn weight and type (i.e. cotton, mohair, wool, etc.). Remember that the description of the yarn weight is only a rough guide and you should always test a yarn first to see if it will achieve the correct tension (gauge).

Magpie Aran: a fisherman medium-weight yarn (100% pure new wool) approx. 150m/164yd per 100g/3½oz hank.

Cotton Glace: a lightweight cotton yarn (100% cotton) approx. 112m/123yd per 50g/1¾oz ball.

Designer DK: a double knitting-weight yarn (100% pure new wool) approx. 115m/125yd per 50g/1¾oz ball.

Handknit DK Cotton: A medium-weight cotton yarn (100% cotton) approx. 85m/90yd per 50g/1¾oz ball.

True 4-ply Botany: a 4-ply yarn (100% pure new wool) approx. 170m/220yd per 50g/1¾oz ball.

DK Tweed: a double knitting weight yarn (100% pure new wool) approx 110m/120yd per 50g/1¾oz ball.

The amount of a substitute yarn needed is determined by the number of metres/yards needed rather than by the number of grams/ounces. If you are unsure when chosing a suitable substitute, ask your yarn shop to advise you.

## TENSION

Each pattern in this book specifies a tension – the number of stitches and rows per centimetre/inch that should be obtained with the given needles, yarn and stitch pattern. Check your tension carefully before commencing work.

Use the same yarn, needles and stitch pattern as those to be used for the main work and knit a sample at least 12.5 cm/5 in square. Smooth out the finished sample on a flat surface but do not stretch it. To check the tension, place a ruler horizontally on the sample and mark 10 cm/4 in across with pins. Count the number of stitches between the pins. To check the row tension, place a ruler horizontally on the sample and mark 10 cm/4 in with pins. Count the number of rows between the pins. If the number of stitches and rows is greater than specified, try again using larger needles; if less, use smaller needles.

The stitch tension is the most important element to get right.

The following terms may be unfamiliar to US readers.

| UK terms | US terms |
| --- | --- |
| Aran wool | *'fisherman' (unbleached wool) yarn* |
| ball band | *yarn wrapper* |
| cast off | *bind off* |
| DK wool | *knitting worsted yarn* |
| double crochet stitch | *single crochet stitch* |
| Make up (garment) | *finish (garment)* |
| rib | *ribbing* |
| stocking stitch | *stockinette stitch* |
| tension | *gauge* |
| waistcoat | *vest* |

In the US balls or hanks of yarn are sold in ounces, not in grams; the weights of the relevant Rowan yarns are given on this page.

In addition, a few specific knitting or crochet terms may be unfamiliar to some readers. The list below explains the abbreviations used in this book to help the reader understand how to follow the various stitches and stages.

## STANDARD ABBREVIATIONS

**alt** = alternate; **beg** = begin(ning); **cont** = continue; **dec** = decreas(e)ing; **foll** = following; **inc** = increas(e)ing; **k** = knit; **m1** = make one by picking up loop lying between st just worked and next st and work into the back of it; **patt** = pattern; **p** = purl; **psso** = pass slipped st over; **rem** = remain(ing); **rep** = repeat; **skpo** = sl one, k1, pass slipped st over; **sl** = slip; **st(s)** = stitch(es); **st st** = stocking stitch; **tbl** = through back of loop(s); **tog** = together; **yb** = yarn back; **yf** = yarn forward; **yon** = yarn over needle; **yrn** = yarn round needle.

## IMPORTANT

Check on ball band for washing instructions. After washing, pat garments into shape and dry flat away from direct heat.

---

Rowan Denim will shrink and fade when it is washed, just like a pair of jeans. Unlike many 'denim look' yarns this uses real indigo dye which only coats the surface of the yarn, leaving a white core that is gradually exposed through washing and wearing.
When washed for the first time the yarn will shrink by up to one-fifth on length; the width, however, will remain the same.
All the necessary adjustments have been made in the instructions for the patterns specially designed for Denim.
The knitted pieces should be washed separately at a temperature of 60-70°C
(140-158°F) before sewing the garment together. The pieces can then be tumble-dried. Dye loss will be greatest during the intial wash; the appearance of the garment will, however, be greatly enhanced with additional washing and wearing.
The cream denim yarn will shrink in the same way but will not fade.

# Tunic Top with Bobble Detail page 8

## MATERIALS
10(11: 11: 12: 13) 50g balls of Rowan Cotton Glacé.
Pair each of 2¾mm (No 12/US 2) and 3¼mm (No 10/US 3) knitting needles.

## TENSION
25 sts and 34 rows to 10cm/4in square over st st on 3¼mm (No 10/US 3) needles.

## ABBREVIATIONS
**mb** = [k1, p1] 3 times then k1 all in next st, pass 2nd, 3rd, 4th, 5th, 6th and 7th st over 1st st.
Also see page 42.

## BACK
With 2¾mm (No 12/US 2) needles cast on 107(112: 122: 132: 142) sts.
K5 rows.
**Next row** K3, [mb, k4] to last 4 sts, mb, k3.
K 3 rows, inc 0(3: 1: 1: 3) sts on last row.
107(115: 123: 133: 145) sts.
Change to 3¼mm (No 10/US 3) needles.
**1st row** K.
**2nd row** K7, p to last 7 sts, k7.
**3rd row** K3, mb, k to last 4 sts, mb, k3.
**4th row** As 2nd row.
**5th and 6th rows** As 1st and 2nd rows.
Rep last 6 rows once more, then work 1st and 2nd rows again.
Cont in st st across all sts until Back measures 32(34: 38: 40: 43)cm/12½(13¼: 15: 15½: 16¾)in from beg, ending with a k row.
**Next row** P5(5: 6: 6: 6), k5, p to last 10(10: 11: 11: 11) sts, k5, p to end.
**Next row** K.
Rep last 2 rows until Back measures 40(44: 48: 52: 55)cm/15¾( 17¼: 19: 20½: 21¾)in from beg, ending with a wrong side row.
Cont in st st across all sts until Back measures 45(49: 53: 57: 60)cm/17¾(19¼: 21: 22½: 23¾)in from beg, ending with a p row.
**Shape Shoulders**
Cast off 19(21: 22: 24: 27) sts at beg of next 2 rows and 20(21: 23: 25: 27) sts at beg of foll 2 rows. Cast off rem 29(31: 33: 35: 37) sts.

## FRONT
Work as given for Back until Front measures 30(32: 36: 38: 41)cm/11¾(12½: 14¼: 14¾: 16)in from beg, ending with a k row.
**Divide for opening**
**Next row** P50(54: 58: 63: 69), k7, turn.
Work on this set of sts only.
**Next row** K.
**Next row** P to last 7 sts, k7.
Rep last 2 rows once more.
**1st row** K3, mb, k to end.
**2nd row** P5(5: 6: 6: 6), k5, p to last 7 sts, k7.
**3rd row** K.
**4th row** As 2nd row.
**5th and 6th rows** As 3rd and 4th rows.
Rep last 6 rows until Front measures 40(44: 48: 52: 55)cm/15¾(17¼: 19: 20½: 21¾)in from beg, ending with a wrong side row.
Keeping patt at opening edge correct and working remainder in st st, cont for a further 1cm/¼in, ending at inside edge.
**Shape Neck**
Cast off 7 sts at beg of next row and 4(4: 4: 5: 5) sts at beg of foll alt row. Dec one st at neck edge on every row until 39(42: 45: 49: 54) sts rem. Cont straight until Front matches Back to shoulder shaping, ending at side edge.
**Shape Shoulder**
Cast off 19(21: 22: 24: 27) sts at beg of next row. Work 1 row. Cast off rem 20(21: 23: 25: 27) sts.
With wrong side facing, rejoin yarn to rem sts, cast on 7 sts, k 7, p to end.
**Next row** K.
**Next row** K7, p to end.
Rep last 2 rows once more.
**1st row** K to last 4 sts, mb, k3.
**2nd row** K7, p to last 10(10: 11: 11: 11) sts, k5, p to end.
**3rd row** K.
**4th row** As 2nd row.
**5th and 6th rows** As 3rd and 4th rows.
Complete to match first side.

## MEASUREMENTS

| To fit age | 3-4 | 4-6 | 6-8 | 8-9 | 9-10 | years |
|---|---|---|---|---|---|---|
| Actual chest | 86 | 92 | 98 | 106 | 116 | cm |
| measurement | 34 | 36 | 38½ | 41½ | 45½ | in |
| Length | 45 | 49 | 53 | 57 | 60 | cm |
| | 17¾ | 19¼ | 21 | 22½ | 23¾ | in |
| Sleeve seam | 28 | 30 | 35 | 38 | 40 | cm |
| | 11 | 12 | 13¾ | 15 | 15¾ | in |

## Tunic Top with Bobble Detail

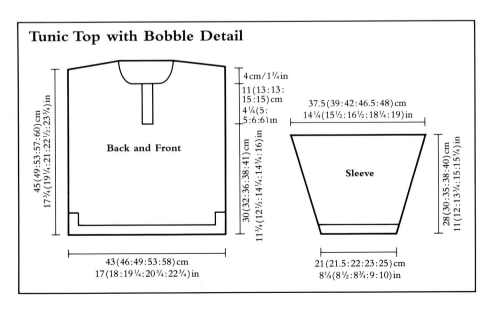

Back and Front

45(49:53:57:60)cm
17¾(19¼:21:22½:23¾)in

43(46:49:53:58)cm
17(18:19¼:20¾:22¾)in

4cm/1¾in
11(13:13:15:15)cm
4¼(5:5:6:6)in

30(32:36:38:41)cm
11¾(12½:14¼:14¾:16)in

37.5(39:42:46.5:48)cm
14¼(15½:16½:18¼:19)in

Sleeve

28(30:35:38:40)cm
11(12:13¾:15:15¾)in

21(21.5:22:23:25)cm
8¼(8½:8¾:9:10)in

43

## SLEEVES

With 2¾mm (No 12/US 2) needles cast on 47(47: 52: 52: 57) sts.
K 5 rows.
**Next row** K3, [mb, k4] to last 4 sts, mb, k3.
K 5 rows, inc 5(7: 4: 6: 5) sts evenly across last row. 52(54: 56: 58: 62) sts.
Change to 3¼mm (No 10/US 3) needles.
Beg with a k row, work in st st, inc one st at each end of 3rd row and every foll 3rd(3rd: 4th: 4th: 4th) row until there are 94(98: 106: 114: 120) sts. Cont straight until Sleeve measures 28(30: 35: 38: 40)cm/11(12: 13¾: 15: 15¾)in from beg, ending with a wrong side row. Cast off.

## COLLAR

With 2¾mm (No 12/US 2) needles cast on 75(81: 87: 93: 99) sts. K 3 rows.
**Next row** K1, k2 tog, k to last 3 sts, k2 tog tbl, k1.
K 4 rows. Rep last 5 rows 4 times more. K 5 rows. Cast off.

## TO MAKE UP

Join shoulder seams. Catch down the 7 cast on sts on wrong side to base of opening. Sew on sleeves, placing centre of sleeves to shoulder seams. Beginning at top of borders, join side seams then sleeve seams. Sew on collar.

# Cable and Bobble Tunic page 9

## MATERIALS

12(13: 14) 50g balls of Rowan Cotton Glace.
Pair each of 3¼mm (No 10/US 3) and 3¾mm (No 9/US 4) knitting needles.
Cable needle.
3 buttons.

## MEASUREMENTS

| To fit age | 3–4 | 6–8 | 9–10 years | |
|---|---|---|---|---|
| Actual chest | 84 | 100 | 117 | cm |
| measurement | 33 | 39½ | 46 | in |
| Length | 44 | 52 | 60 | cm |
| | 17¼ | 20½ | 23¾ | in |
| Sleeve seam | 28 | 35 | 41 | cm |
| | 11 | 13¾ | 16 | in |

## TENSION

29 sts and 36 rows to 10cm/4in square over pattern on 3¾mm (No 9/US 4) needles.

## ABBREVIATIONS

**C4B** = sl next 2 sts onto cable needle and leave at back of work, k2, then k2 from cable needle;
**Cr3L** = sl next 2 sts onto cable needle and leave at front of work, p1, then k2 from cable needle;
**Cr3R** = sl next st onto cable needle and leave at back of work, k2, then p1 from cable needle;
**mb** = pick up loop lying between st just worked and next st and work into front, back, front, back and front of the loop, then pass 2nd, 3rd, 4th and 5th st over 1st st.
Also see page 42.

## BACK

With 3¼mm (No 10/US 3) needles cast on 122(146: 170) sts.
**1st rib row (right side)** [P2, k2, p1, k4, p1, k2] to last 2 sts, p2.
**2nd rib row** K2, [p2, k1, p4, k1, p2, k2] to end.
**3rd rib row** [P1, mb, p1, pass bobble st over the p st just worked, k2, p1, C4B, p1, k2] to last 2 sts, p2.
**4th rib row** As 2nd row.
Rib a further 14 rows.
Change to 3¾mm (No 9/US 4) needles.
**1st row** P1, [mb, p1, pass bobble st over the p st just worked, p3, C4B, p4] to last st, p1.
**2nd row** K5, [p4, k8] to last 9 sts, p4, k5.
**3rd row** P4, [Cr3R, Cr3L, p6] to last 10 sts, Cr3R, Cr3L, p4.
**4th row** K4, [p6, k6] to last 10 sts, p6, k4.
**5th row** P1, [mb, p1, pass bobble st over the p st just worked, p1, Cr3R, p2, Cr3L, p2] to last st, p1.
**6th row** K3, [p8, k4] to last 11 sts, p8, k3.
**7th row** P2, [Cr3R, p4, Cr3L, p2] to end.
**8th row** K2, [p10, k2] to end.
**9th row** P1, [Cr3R, p6, Cr3L] to last st, p1.

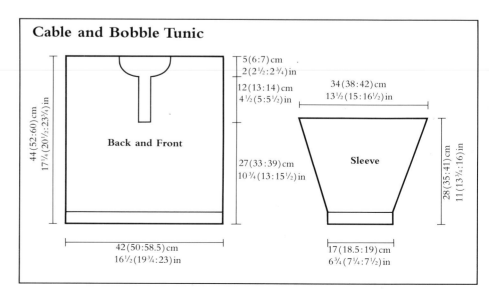

**Cable and Bobble Tunic**

Back and Front

44(52:60)cm
17¼(20½:23¾)in

42(50:58.5)cm
16½(19¾:23)in

5(6:7)cm
2(2½:2¾)in

12(13:14)cm
4½(5:5½)in

34(38:42)cm
13½(15:16½)in

27(33:39)cm
10¾(13:15½)in

Sleeve

28(35:41)cm
11(13¾:16)in

17(18.5:19)cm
6¾(7¼:7½)in

**10th row** K1, p to last st, k1.
**11th row** P1, [Cr3L, p6, Cr3R] to last st, p1.
**12th row** As 8th row.
**13th row** P2, [Cr3L, p4, Cr3R, p2] to end.
**14th row** As 6th row.
**15th row** P1, [mb, p1, pass bobble st over the p st just worked, p1, Cr3L, p2, Cr3R, p2] to last st, p1.
**16th row** As 4th row.
**17th row** P4, [Cr3L, Cr3R, p6] to last 10 sts, Cr3L, Cr3R, p4.
**18th row** As 2nd row.
**19th and 20th rows** As 1st and 2nd rows.
**21st row** P5, [k4, p8] to last 9 sts, k4, p5.
**22nd row** As 2nd row.
These 22 rows form patt. Cont in patt until Back measures approximately 27(33: 39)cm/10¾(13: 15½)in from beg, ending with 14th patt row. Mark each end of last row. ★★
Omitting making first bobble throughout, cont in patt until Back measures 44(52: 60)cm/17¼(20½: 23¾)in from beg, ending with a wrong side row.

**Shape Shoulders**
**Next row** Cast off 42(52: 62), patt to last 42(52: 62) sts, cast of these sts.
Leave rem 38(42: 46) sts on a holder.

## FRONT
Work as given for Back to ★★. Omitting making first bobble throughout, work as follows:

**Divide for Opening**
**Next row** Patt 58(70: 82), cast off next 6 sts, patt to end.
Cont on last set of sts only. Keeping patt correct, work a further 12(13: 14)cm/4½(5: 5½)in, ending at inside edge.

**Shape Neck**
Cast off 8(9: 10) sts at beg of next row. Dec one st at neck edge on next 5 rows then on every foll alt row until 42(52: 62) sts rem. Cont straight until Front matches Back to shoulder shaping, ending with a wrong side row. Cast off.
With wrong side facing, rejoin yarn to rem sts and patt to end. Complete as given for first side.

## SLEEVES
With 3¼mm (No 10/US 3) needles cast on 50(54: 56) sts.
**1st rib row (right side)** P0(0: 1), k0(2: 2), p2, [k2, p1, k4, p1, k2, p2] to last 0(2: 3) sts, k0(2: 2), p0(0: 1).
**2nd rib row** K0(0: 1), p0(2: 2), [k2, p2, k1, p4, k1, p2] to last 2(4: 5) sts, k2, p0(2: 2), k0(0: 1).
These 2 rows set position of rib. Cont in rib to match Back, work a further 16 rows. Change to 3¾mm (No 9/US 4) needles.
**1st row** P1(3: 4), [mb, p1, pass bobble st over the p st just worked, p3, C4B, p4] to last 1(3: 4) sts, mb, p1, pass bobble st over the p st just worked, p0(2: 3).
**2nd row** K5(7: 8), p4, [k8, p4] to last 5(7: 8) sts, k5(7: 8).
These 2 rows set position of patt. Cont in patt, inc one st at each end of next row and every foll 3rd row until there are 98(110: 122) sts, working inc sts into patt. Cont straight until Sleeve measures 28(35: 41)cm/11(13¾: 16)in from beg, ending with a wrong side row. Cast off.

## NECKBAND
Join shoulder seams.
With 3¼mm (No 10/US 3) needles and right side facing, k up 21(24: 27) sts up right front neck, k6(2: 2), k2 tog, [k4(4: 3), k2 tog] 4(6: 8) times, k6(2: 2) across back neck, k up 21(24: 27) sts down left front neck. 75(83: 91) sts. K 6 rows. Cast off.

## BUTTON BAND
With 3¼mm (No 10/US 3) needles and right side facing, k up 30(33: 36) sts along left edge of front opening, including neckband. K 10 rows. Cast off.

## BUTTONHOLE BAND
With 3¼mm (No 10/US 3) needles and right side facing, k up 30(33: 36) sts along right edge of front opening, including neckband. K 3 rows.
★★★ **Next row** K10(11: 12), turn.
Work on this set of sts only.
**Next row** K2 tog, k to last 2 sts, k2 tog tbl.
**Next row** K.
Rep last 2 rows until 2(3: 2) sts rem. Work 2(3: 2) tog and fasten off. With right side facing, rejoin yarn to rem sts and rep from ★★★ twice more.

## TO MAKE UP
Sew on sleeves between markers. Join side and sleeve seams. Catch down row end edge of button band to base of opening. Push large knitting needle through sts on each point of buttonhole band thus forming buttonhole. Sew on button

# Cabled, Zipped Jacket with Collar page 12

## MATERIALS
19(22) 50g balls of Rowan DK Handknit Cotton.
Pair each of 3¼mm (No 10/US 3) and 4mm (No 8/US 6) knitting needles.
Cable needle.
45(55)cm/18(22)in long open ended zip fastener.

## MATERIALS

| To fit age | 4-6 | 6-8 years |
|---|---|---|
| Actual chest | 101 | 119 cm |
| measurement | 40 | 47 in |
| Length | 56 | 66 cm |
| | 22 | 26 in |
| Sleeve seam | 30 | 38 cm |
| | 12 | 15 in |

## TENSION
27 sts and 29 rows to 10cm/4in square over pattern on 4mm (No 8/US 6) needles.

## ABBREVIATIONS
**Tw4L** = sl next 3 sts onto cable needle and leave at front of work, k1, then k1 tbl, p1, k1 tbl from cable needle;
**Tw4R** = sl next st onto cable needle and leave at back of work, k1 tbl, p1, k1 tbl, then k1 from cable needle;
**mb** = [k1, yf, k1, yf, k1] all in next st, turn, p5, turn, k3, k2 tog, then pass 2nd, 3rd and 4th st over first st.
Also see page 42.

## PANEL A
Worked over 23 sts.
**1st row** (wrong side) K8, p1, k1, p3, k1, p1, k8.
**2nd row** P7, Tw4R, k1 tbl, Tw4L, p7.
**3rd row** K7, p1, [k1, p1] 4 times, k7.
**4th row** P6, Tw4R, k1, k1 tbl, k1, Tw4L, p6.
**5th row** K6, p1, k1, p1, [k2, p1] twice, k1, p1, k6.

**6th row** P5, Tw4R, k2, k1tbl, k2, Tw4L, p5.
**7th row** K5, p1, k1, p2, k2, p1, k2, p2, k1, p1, k5.
**8th row** P4, Tw4R, k1 tbl, [k2, k1tbl] twice, Tw4L, p4.
**9th row** K4, p1, [k1, p1] twice, [k2, p1] twice, [k1, p1] twice, k4.
**10th row** P3, Tw4R, k1, k1 tbl, [k2, k1 tbl] twice, k1, Tw4L, p3.
**11th row** K3, p1, k1, p1, [k2, p1] 4 times, k1, p1, k3.
**12th row** P2, Tw4R, k2, [k1 tbl, k2] 3 times, Tw4L, p2.
**13th row** K2, p1, k1, p1, k3, p1, [k2, p1] twice, k3, p1, k1, p1, k2.
**14th row** P2, k1 tbl, p1, k1 tbl, k3, mb, [k2, mb] twice, k3, k1 tbl, p1, k1 tbl, p2.
**15th row** K2, p1, k1, p1, k3, p1 tbl, [k2, p1 tbl] twice, k3, p1, k1, p1, k2.
**16th row** P2, k1 tbl, p1, k1 tbl, p3, k1 tbl, p1, k3 tbl, p1, k1 tbl, p3, k1 tbl, p1, k1 tbl, p2.
These 16 rows form patt.

## PANEL B
Worked over 13 sts.
**1st row (wrong side)** P1, k2, [p1, k1] 3 times, p1, k2, p1.
**2nd row** K1 tbl, p2, sl next 3 sts onto cable needle and leave at front of work, [k1 tbl, p1] twice, then k1 tbl, p1, k1 tbl from cable needle, p2, k1 tbl.
**3rd row** As 1st row.
**4th row** K1 tbl, p2, k1 tbl, [p1, k1 tbl] 3 times, p2, k1 tbl.
**5th to 10th rows** Rep 3rd and 4th rows 3 times.
These 10 rows form patt.

## BACK
With 3¼mm (No 10/US 3) needles cast on 107(127) sts.
**1st rib row (right side)** K1 tbl, [p1, k1 tbl] to end.
**2nd rib row** P1, [k1, p1] to end.
Rep last 2 rows until welt measures 5cm/2in, ending with a wrong side row.
**1st size only**
**Inc row** [Rib 3, m1] twice, rib 2, m1, rib 7, m1, rib 3, m1, rib 2, m1, ★ rib 2, m1, rib 7, m1, rib 2, m1, rib 3, m1, rib 2, m1, rib 7, m1, rib 3, m1, rib 2, m1; rep from ★ twice more, rib 3. 137 sts.
Change to 4mm (No 8/US 6) needles.
**1st row (wrong side)** K2, p1, work 1st row of panel A, [work 1st row of panel B, then panel A] 3 times, p1, k2.
**2nd row** P2, k1 tbl, work 2nd row of panel A, [work 2nd row of panel B, then panel A] 3 times, k1 tbl, p2.
**2nd size only**
**Inc row** Rib 4, ★m1, rib 7, [m1, rib 2] twice, m1, rib 3, m1, rib 7, m1, rib 2, m1, rib 3, m1, rib 2; rep from ★ 3 times more, m1, rib 7, m1, rib 4. (161) sts.
Change to 4mm (No 8/US 6) needles.
**1st row (wrong side)** K2, work 1st row of panel B, [work 1st row of panel A, then panel B] 4 times, k2.
**2nd row** P2, work 2nd row of panel B, [work 2nd row of panel A, then panel B] 4 times, p2.
**Both sizes**
These 2 rows set position of panels. Cont in patt until Back measures 56(66)cm/22(26)in from beg, ending with a wrong side row.

## Shape Shoulders
Cast off 24(30) sts at beg of next 4 rows.
Cast off rem 41 sts.

## LEFT FRONT
With 3¼mm (No 10/US 3) needles cast on 52(62) sts.
**1st rib row (right side)** K1 tbl, [p1, k1 tbl] to last 3 sts, k3.
**2nd rib row** K3, p1, [k1, p1] to end.
Rep last 2 rows until welt measures 5cm/2in, ending with a wrong side row.
**1st size**
**Inc row** [Rib 3, m1] twice, rib 2, m1, rib 7, m1, rib 3, m1, [rib 2, m1] twice, rib 7, m1, rib 2, m1, rib 3, m1, rib 2, m1, rib 7, m1, rib 3, m1, rib 2, m1, rib1, k3. 66 sts.
Change to 4mm (No 8/US 6) needles.
**1st row (wrong side)** K3, p1, work 1st row of panel A, then panel B and panel A, p1, k2.
**2nd row** P2, k1 tbl, work 2nd row of panel A, then panel B and panel A, k1 tbl, k3.
**2nd size**
**Inc row** Rib 2, ★ rib 2, m1, rib 7, [m1, rib 2] twice, m1, rib 3, m1, rib 7, m1, rib 2, m1, rib 3, m1; rep from ★ once more, rib 1, k3. (78) sts.
Change to 4mm (No 8/US 6) needles.
**1st row (wrong side)** K3, p1, [work 1st row of panel A, then panel B] twice, k2.
**2nd row** P2, [work 2nd row of panel B, then panel A] twice, k1 tbl, k3.
**Both sizes**
These 2 rows set position of panels. Cont in patt until Front measures 45(55)cm/17¾ (21¾)in from beg, end with wrong side row.
## Shape Neck
**Next row** Patt to last 3 sts, turn; leave the 3 sts on a safety pin.
Keeping patt correct, dec one st at neck edge on next 4 rows, then on every alt row until 48(60) sts rem. Cont straight until Front matches Back to shoulder shaping, ending with a wrong side row.
## Shape Shoulder
Cast off 24(30) sts at beg of next row. Work 1 row. Cast off rem 24(30) sts.

## RIGHT FRONT
With 3¼mm (No 10/US 3) needles cast on 52(62) sts.
**1st rib row (right side)** K3, k1tbl, [p1, k1 tbl] to end.
**2nd rib row** P1, [k1, p1] to last 3 sts, k3.
Rep last 2 rows until welt measures 5cm/2in, ending with a wrong side row.
**1st size**
**Inc row** K3, rib 1, m1, rib 2, m1, rib 3, m1, rib 7, m1, rib 2, m1, rib 3, m1, rib 2, m1, rib 7, m1, [rib 2, m1] twice, rib 3, m1, rib 7, m1, rib 2, [m1, rib 3] twice. 66 sts.
Change to 4mm (No 8/US 6) needles.
**1st row (wrong side)** K2, p1, work 1st row of panel A, then panel B and panel A, p1, k3.
**2nd row** K3, k1 tbl, work 2nd row of panel A, then panel B and panel A, k1 tbl, p2.
**2nd size**
**Inc row** K3, rib 1, ★m1, rib 2, m1, rib 3, m1, rib 7, [m1, rib 2] twice, m1, rib 3, m1, rib 7, m1, rib 2; rep from ★ once more, rib 2. (78) sts.
Change to 4mm (No 8/US 6) needles.
**1st row (wrong side)** K2, [work 1st row of panel B, then panel A] twice, p1, k3.
**2nd row** K3, k1 tbl, [work 2nd row of panel A, then panel B] twice, p2.
**Both sizes**
These 2 rows set position of panels.
Complete as given for Left Front, reversing shapings.

## SLEEVES
With 3¼mm (No 10/US 3) needles cast on 49 sts.
**1st rib row (right side)** P1, [k1 tbl, p1] to end.
**2nd rib row** K1, [p1, k1] to end.
Rep last 2 rows until cuff measures 5cm/2in, ending with a wrong side row.
**Inc row** Rib 2, m1, rib 3, m1, rib 2, m1, rib 7, m1, rib 3, m1, [rib 2, m1] twice, rib 7, m1, rib 2, m1, rib 3, m1, rib 2, m1, rib 7, m1, rib 3, [m1, rib 2] twice. 63 sts.
Change to 4mm (No 8/US 6) needles.
**1st row (wrong side)** K1, p1, work 1st row of panel A, then panel B and panel A, p1, k1.

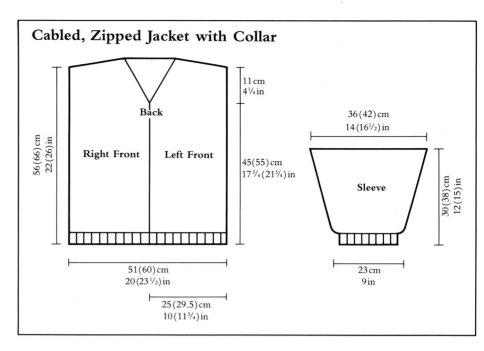

**Cabled, Zipped Jacket with Collar**

Back
Right Front  Left Front

56(66)cm 22(26)in

11 cm 4¼ in

45(55) cm 17¾(21¾) in

51(60) cm 20(23½) in

25(29.5) cm 10(11¾) in

36(42) cm 14(16½) in

Sleeve

30(38) cm 12(15) in

23 cm 9 in

**2nd row** P1, k1 tbl, work 2nd row of panel A, then panel B and panel A, k1 tbl, p1. These 2 rows set position of panels. Cont in patt, inc one st at each end of next row and 10 foll 3rd rows, working inc sts into panel B patt. Work in patt, inc one st at each end of 6(11) foll 4th rows, working inc sts into reverse st st. 97(107) sts. Cont straight until Sleeve measures 30(38)cm/12(15)in from beg, ending with a wrong side row. Cast off.

## COLLAR
### Left side
With 4mm (No 8/US 6) needles, rejoin yarn at inside edge to the 3sts on Left Front safety pin, cast on 4, p1, k2, p1, k3.
**Next row** K3, k1 tbl, p2, k1 tbl.
**Next row** Cast on 3, [k1, p1] twice, k2, p1, k3.
**Next row** K3, k1 tbl, p2, [k1 tbl, p1] twice.
**Next row** Cast on 3, p1, [k1, p1] 3 times, k2, p1, k3.
**Next row** K3, k1 tbl, p2, k1 tbl, [p1, k1 tbl] 3 times.
**Next row** Cast on 3, work 7th row of panel B, k3.
**Next row** K3, work 8th row of panel B.
**Next row** Cast on 3, p1, k2 (last 3 sts of 15th row of panel A), work 9th row of panel B, k3.

**Next row** K3, work 10th row of panel B, p2, k1 tbl (first 3 sts of 16th row of panel A). Cont in patt, inc one st at inside edge on every row until there are 44 sts, then on 2 foll alt rows, working inc sts into panel A, then panel B. 46 sts. Work 1 row straight. Leave these sts on a holder.
### Right Side
With 4mm (No 8/US 6) needles, rejoin yarn at inside edge to the 3 sts on Right Front safety pin, cast on 4 sts, K1 tbl, p2, k1 tbl, k3.
**Next row** K3, p1, k2, p1.
**Next row** Cast on 3, [p1, k1 tbl] twice, p2, k1 tbl, k3.
**Next row** K3, p1, k2, [p1, k1] twice.
**Next row** Cast on 3, k1 tbl, [p1, k1 tbl] 3 times, p2, k1 tbl, k3.
**Next row** K3, p1, k2, p1, [k1, p1] 3 times.
**Next row** Cast on 3, work 8th row of panel B, k3.
**Next row** K3, work 9th row of panel B.
**Next row** Cast on 3, k1 tbl, p2 (last 3 sts of 16th row of chart A), work 10th row of panel B, k3.
Cont in patt, inc one st at inside edge on every row until there are 44 sts, then on 2 foll alt rows, working inc sts into panel A, then panel B. 46 sts. Work 1 row.

**Next row** Patt to end, cast on 35, patt across sts of left side. 127 sts.
Patt 32 rows.
**Next row** Patt 17 sts and sl these sts onto a holder, patt to last 17 sts, turn; leave the last 17 sts on a holder.
Work on centre 93 sts only. Keeping patt correct, dec one st at each end of next 5 rows. Cast off 3 sts at beg of next 4 row, 4 sts at beg of foll 4 rows and 5 sts at beg of foll 8 rows. Cast off rem 15 sts.
Rejoin yarn at inside edge to one set of 17 sts and cont in patt until border fits round shaped edge of collar to centre. Leave these sts. Work other side to match. With right sides of border together, cast off together border sts.

## TO MAKE UP
Join shoulder seams. Sew collar border in place, then sew on collar. Sew on sleeves, placing centre of sleeves to shoulder seams. Join side and sleeve seams. Sew in zip fastner.

# Ribbed Denim Sweater page 13

## MEASUREMENTS

| To fit age | 3-4 | 4-6 | 6-8 | 8-9 | 9-10 | years |
|---|---|---|---|---|---|---|
| *The following measurements are after the garment has been washed to the instructions given on ball band.* | | | | | | |
| Actual chest | 82 | 87 | 97 | 102 | 112 | cm |
| measurement | 32 | 34 | 38 | 40 | 44 | in |
| Length | 44 | 48 | 53 | 57 | 62 | cm |
| | 17¼ | 19 | 21 | 22½ | 24½ | in |
| Sleeve seam | 28 | 30 | 35 | 38 | 43 | cm |
| | 11 | 12 | 13¾ | 15 | 17 | in |

## MATERIALS
12(14: 15: 17: 19) 50g balls of Rowan Denim.
Pair each of 3¼mm (No 10/US 3), 3¾mm (No 9/US 4) and 4mm (No 8/US 6) knitting needles.

## TENSION
20 sts and 30 rows to 10cm/4in square over rib pattern on 4mm (No 8/US 6) needles.

## ABBREVIATIONS
See page 42.

## BACK
With 3¾mm (No 9/US 4) needles cast on 82(87: 97: 102: 112) sts.
**1st rib row (right side)** K2, [p3, k2] to end.
**2nd rib row** P.
These 2 rows form rib patt. Rep last 2 rows once more.
Change to 4mm (No 8/US 6) needles.
Cont in patt until Back measures 31(35: 38: 41: 46)cm/12(13¾: 15: 16: 18)in from beg. Mark each end of last row. Cast on one st at beg of next 2 rows. 84(89: 99: 104: 114) sts.
Cont in patt until Back measures 50(55: 60: 65: 71)cm/19½(21½: 23½: 25½: 28)in from beg, ending with a right side row.
### Shape Neck
**Next row** Patt 33(34: 39: 42: 47), turn. Work on this set of sts only. Keeping patt correct, cast off 2(2: 3: 3: 4) sts at beg of next row and foll alt row. 29(30: 33: 36: 39) sts.
### Shape Shoulder
Cast off 10(10: 11: 12: 13) sts at beg of next row and foll alt row. Work 1 row. Cast off rem 9(10: 11: 12: 13) sts.
With wrong side facing, slip centre 18(21: 21: 20: 20) sts onto a holder, rejoin yarn to rem sts, cast off 2(2: 3: 3: 4) sts, patt to end. Patt 1 row. Cast off 2(2: 3: 3: 4) sts at beg of next row.
### Shape Shoulder
Cast off 10(10: 11: 12: 13) sts at beg of next row and foll alt row. Work 1 row. Cast off rem 9(10: 11: 12: 13) sts.

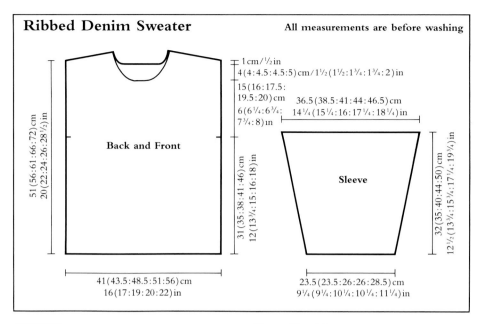

## Ribbed Denim Sweater

**All measurements are before washing**

*Back and Front diagram:*
- 51(56:61:66:72)cm / 20(22:24:26:28½)in
- 41(43.5:48.5:51:56)cm / 16(17:19:20:22)in
- 31(35:38:41:46)cm / 12(13¾:15:16:18)in
- 1cm/½in
- 4(4:4.5:4.5:5)cm/1½(1½:1¾:1¾:2)in
- 15(16:17.5:19.5:20)cm / 6(6¼:6¾:7¾:8)in
- 36.5(38.5:41:44:46.5)cm / 14¼(15¼:16:17¼:18¼)in

*Sleeve diagram:*
- 32(35:40:44:50)cm / 12½(13¾:15¾:17¼:19¾)in
- 23.5(23.5:26:26:28.5)cm / 9¼(9¼:10¼:10¼:11¼)in

### FRONT

Work as given for Back until Front measures 46(51: 55.5: 60.5: 66)cm/18(20: 21¾: 23¾: 26)in from beg, ending with a right side row.

### Shape Neck

**Next row** Patt 35(36: 40: 43: 47), turn. Work on this set of sts only. Dec one st at neck edge on next 3 rows, then on 3(3: 4: 4: 5) foll alt rows. 29(30: 33: 36: 39) sts. Cont straight until Front matches Back to shoulder shaping, ending at side edge.

### Shape Shoulder

Cast off 10(10: 11: 12: 13) sts at beg of next row and foll alt row. Work 1 row. Cast off rem 9(10: 11: 12: 13) sts.

With wrong side facing, slip centre 14(17: 19: 18: 20) sts onto a holder, rejoin yarn to rem sts and patt to end. Complete as given for first side.

### SLEEVES

With 3¾mm (No 9/US 4) needles cast on 47(47: 52: 52: 57) sts.
Work in rib patt as given for Back for 6cm/2½in.
Change to 4mm (No 8/US 6) needles.
Cont in patt, inc one st at each end of 5th row and every foll 5th(5th: 6th: 5th: 6th) row until there are 73(77: 82: 88: 93) sts, working inc sts into patt. Cont straight until Sleeve measures 32(35: 40: 44: 50)cm/12½(13¾: 15¾: 17¼: 19¾)in from beg, ending with a wrong side row. Cast off.

### NECKBAND

Join right shoulder seam.
With 3¼mm (No 10/US 3) needles and right side facing, k up 16(16: 18: 18: 20) sts down left front neck, k centre front sts, k up 16(16: 18: 18: 20) sts up right front neck, 9(9: 10: 11: 13) sts down right back neck, k centre back sts, k up 9(9: 10: 11: 13) sts up left back neck. 82(88: 96: 96: 106) sts. Work 9(9: 11: 13: 13) rows in k1, p1 rib. Beg with a k row, work 8(8: 10: 10: 12) rows in st st. Cast off loosely.

### TO MAKE UP

Join left shoulder and neckband seam, reversing seam on st st section of neckband. Sew on sleeves between markers. Join side and sleeve seams.

# Cream Denim Sweater page 14

### MATERIALS

16(17: 18) 50g balls of Rowan Denim.
Pair of 3¼mm (No 10/US 3), 3¾mm (No 9/US 4) and 4mm (No 8/US 6) knitting needles.
Cable needle.

### MEASUREMENTS

| To fit age | 4-6 | 6-8 | 8-10 years |
|---|---|---|---|

*The following measurements are after the garment has been washed to the instructions given on ball band.*

| | | | | |
|---|---|---|---|---|
| Actual chest | 104 | 118 | 124 | cm |
| measurement | 41 | 46½ | 49 | in |
| Length | 51 | 56 | 61 | cm |
| | 20 | 22 | 24 | in |
| Sleeve seam | 29 | 33 | 39 | cm |
| | 11½ | 13 | 15½ | in |

### TENSION

21 sts and 30 rows to 10cm/4in square over moss st on 4mm (No 8/US 6) needles before washing.

### ABBREVIATIONS

**C2B** = sl next st onto cable needle and leave at back of work, k1, then k1 from cable needle;
**C2F** = sl next st onto cable needle and leave at front of work, k1, then k1 from cable needle;
**C3B** = sl next st onto cable needle and leave at back of work, k2, then k1 from cable needle;
**C3F** = sl next 2 sts onto cable needle and leave at front of work, k1, then k2 from cable needle;
**C6F** = sl next 3 sts onto cable needle and leave at front of work, k3, then k3 from cable needle;
**Cr2L** = sl next st onto cable needle and leave at front of work, p1, then k1 from cable needle;
**Cr2R** = sl next st onto cable needle and leave at back of work, k1, then p1 from cable needle;
**Cr3L** = sl next 2 sts onto cable needle and leave at front of work, p1, then k2 from cable needle;
**Cr3R** = sl next st onto cable needle and leave at back of work, k2, then p1 from cable needle
Also see page 42.

## PANEL A

Worked over 8 sts.
**1st row (right side)** K6, p1, k1.
**2nd row** P2, k1, p5.
**3rd row** K4, [p1, k1] twice.
**4th row** P2, k1, p1, k1, p3.
**5th row** K2, [p1, k1] 3 times.
**6th row** P2, [k1, p1] 3 times.
**7th row** As 5th row.
**8th row** As 4th row.
**9th row** As 3rd row.
**10th row** As 2nd row.
These 10 rows form patt.

## PANEL B

Worked over 18 sts.
**1st row (right side)** P5, k8, p5.
**2nd row** K5, p8, k5.
**3rd row** P4, Cr2R, k6, Cr2L, p4.
**4th row** K4, p1, k1, p6, k1, p1, k4.
**5th row** P3, Cr2R, p1, k6, p1, Cr2L, p3.
**6th row** K3, p1, k2, p6, k2, p1, k3.
**7th row** P2, Cr2R, p2, C6F, p2, Cr2L, p2.
**8th row** K2, p1, k3, p6, k3, p1, k2.
**9th row** P1, Cr2R, p3, k6, p3, Cr2L, p1.
**10th row** K1, p1, k4, p6, k4, p1, k1.
**11th row** P1, Cr2L, p3, k6, p3, Cr2R, p1.
**12th row** As 8th row.
**13th row** P2, Cr2L, p2, C6F, p2, Cr2R, p2.
**14th row** As 6th row.
**15th row** P3, Cr2L, p1, k6, p1, Cr2R, p3.
**16th row** As 4th row.
**17th row** P4, Cr2L, k6, Cr2R, p4.
**18th row** K5, p8, k5.
Rows 3 to 18 form patt.

## PANEL C

Worked over 8 sts.
**1st row (right side)** K1, p1, k6.
**2nd row** P5, k1, p2.
**3rd row** [K1, p1] twice, k4.
**4th row** P3, k1, p1, k1, p2.
**5th row** [K1, p1] 3 times, k2.
**6th row** [P1, k1] 3 times, p2.
**7th row** As 5th row.
**8th row** As 4th row.
**9th row** As 3rd row.
**10th row** As 2nd row.
These 10 rows form patt.

## PANEL D

Worked over 14 sts.
**1st row (right side)** P3, k8, p3.
**2nd row** K3, p8, k3.
**3rd row** P4, C3B, Cr3L, p4.
**4th row** K4, p3, k1, p2, k4.
**5th row** P3, Cr3R, k1, p1, C3F, p3.
**6th row** K3, p2, [k1, p1] twice, p2, k3.
**7th row** P2, C3B, [p1, k1] twice, Cr3L, p2.
**8th row** K2, p3, [k1, p1] twice, k1, p2, k2.
**9th row** P1, Cr3R, [k1, p1] 3 times, C3F, p1.
**10th row** K1, p2, [k1, p1] 4 times, p2, k1.
**11th row** P1, Cr3L, [k1, p1] 3 times, Cr3R, p1.
**12th row** As 8th row.
**13th row** P2, Cr3L, [p1, k1] twice, Cr3R, p2.
**14th row** As 6th row.
**15th row** P3, Cr3L, k1, p1, Cr3R, p3.
**16th row** As 4th row.
**17th row** P4, Cr3L, Cr3R, p4.
**18th row** K5, p4, k3.
**19th row** P3, sl next 2 sts onto cable needle and leave at back of work, k2, then k2 from cable needle, sl next 2 sts onto cable needle and leave at front of work, k2, then k2 from cable needle, p3.
**20th row** K3, p8, k3.
**21st row** P3, k8, p3.
**22nd row** As 20th row.
**23rd and 24th rows** As 19th and 20th rows.
These 24 rows form patt.

## BACK AND FRONT ALIKE

With 3¾mm (No 9/US 4) needles cast on 116(128: 140) sts.
**1st row (right side)** K41(47: 53), work 1st row of panels A, B and C, k to end.
**2nd row** P2, [k2, p4] 6(7: 8) times, k2, p1, work 2nd row of panels C, B and A, [k2, p4] 6(7: 8) times, k2, p3.
**3rd row** K2, [C2F, k4] 6(7: 8) times, C2F, k1, patt 34 sts as set, [C2F, k4] 6(7: 8) times, C2F, k3.
**4th row** P2, [k1, p1, k1, p3] 6(7: 8) times, k1, p1, k1, patt 34, [k1, p1, k1, p3] 6(7: 8) times, k1, p1, k1, p2.

**5th row** K3, [C2F, k4] 6(7: 8) times, C2F, patt 34, k1, [C2F, k4] 6(7: 8) times, C2F, k2.
**6th row** P3, [k2, p4] 6(7: 8) times, k2, patt 34, p1, [k2, p4] 6(7: 8) times, k2, p2.
**7th row** K41(47: 53), patt 34, k to end.
**8th row** As 6th row.
**9th row** K3, [C2B, k4] 6(7: 8) times, C2B, patt 34, k1, [C2B, k4] 6(7: 8) times, C2B, k2.
**10th row** As 4th row.
**11th row** K2, [C2B, k4] 6(7: 8) times, C2B, k1, patt 34, [C2B, k4] 6(7: 8) times, C2B, k3.
**12th row** P2, [k2, p4] 6(7: 8) times, k2, p1, patt 34, [k2, p4] 6(7: 8) times, k2, p3.
Work a further 37 rows as set.
**Inc row** [Patt 8(9: 16), m1] 5(5: 3) times, patt 36(38: 44), [m1, patt 8(9: 16)] 5(5: 3) times. 126(138: 146) sts.
Change to 4mm (No 8/US 6) needles.
**1st row (right side)** [K1, p1] 3(2: 4) times, [work 1st row of panel A] 0(1: 1) time, [work 3rd row of panel B, work 1st row of panels C, D and A] twice, work 3rd row of panel B, [work 1st row of panel C] 0(1: 1) time, [p1, k1] 3(2: 4) times.
**2nd row** [K1, p1] 3(2: 4) times, [work 2nd row of panel C] 0(1: 1) time, [ work 4th row of panel B, work 2nd row of panel A, D and C] twice, work 4th row of panel B, [work 2nd row of panel A] 0(1: 1) time, [p1, k1] 3(2: 4) times.
These 2 rows set position of panels. Cont in patt until work measures 52(57: 63)cm/20 1/2(22 1/2: 24 3/4)in from beg, ending with a wrong side row.
**Shape Shoulders**
Cast off 15(17: 18) sts at beg of next 4 rows and 15(17: 19) sts at beg of foll 2 rows.
Leave rem 36 sts on a holder.

## SLEEVES

With 3¼mm (No 10/US 3) needles cast on 43(43: 49) sts.
**1st row** (right side) K.
**2nd row** P2, [k2, p4] to last 5 sts, k2, p3.
**3rd row** K2, [C2F, k4] to last 5 sts, C2F, k3.
**4th row** P2, [k1, p1, k1, p3] to last 5 sts, k1, p1, k1, p2.
**5th row** K3, [C2F, k4] to last 4 sts, C2F, k2.
**6th row** P3, [k2, p4] to last 4 sts, k2, p2.
**7th row** K.
**8th row** As 6th row.
**9th row** K3, [C2B, k4] to last 4 sts, C2B, k2.
**10th row** As 4th row.
**11th row** K2, [C2B, k4] to last 5 sts, C2B, k3.
**12th row** As 2nd row.
Work a further 5 rows as set.
**Inc row** Patt 1(1: 3), [m1, rib 2] to end. 64(64: 72) sts.
Change to 4mm (No 8/US 6) needles.
**1st row** Work last 1(1: 5) sts of 1st row of panel C, work 1st row of panels D, A, B, C and D, work first 1(1: 5) sts of 1st row of panel A.
**2nd row** Work last 1(1: 5) sts of 2nd row of panel A, work 2nd row of panels D, C, B, A and D, work first 1(1: 5) sts of 2nd row of panel C.
These 2 rows set position of panels. Cont in patt, inc one st at each end of 7th row and every foll 6th(6th: 7th) row until there are 84(92: 98) sts, working inc sts into panel A and C as set, then into moss st. Cont straight until Sleeve measures 34(38: 45)cm/13½(15: 17¾)in from beg, ending with a wrong side row.

---

## Cream Denim Sweater

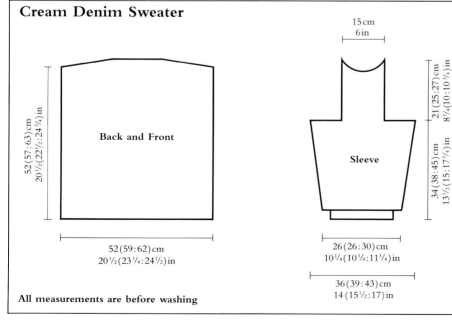

**Back and Front**

52(57: 63)cm
20½(22½: 24¾)in

52(59: 62)cm
20½(23¼: 24½)in

15 cm
6 in

21(25: 27)cm
8¼(10: 10¾)in

34(38: 45)cm
13½(15: 17¾)in

**Sleeve**

26(26: 30)cm
10¼(10¼: 11¾)in

36(39: 43)cm
14(15½: 17)in

**All measurements are before washing**

**Shape Saddle**
Cast off 24(28: 31) sts at beg of next 2 rows.
Patt a further 18(22: 24)cm/7(8¾: 9½)in on
rem 36 sts.
**Shape Neck**
**Next row** Patt 8, work 2 tog, turn.
Work on this set of sts only. Dec one st at
inside edge on every row until 2 sts rem.
Work 2 tog and fasten off.
With right side facing, slip centre 16 sts onto
a holder, rejoin yarn, work 2 tog and patt to
end. Complete as given for first side.

**NECKBAND**
With 3¼mm (No 10/US 3) needles and
right side facing, k up 10 sts down first side
of left sleeve, k centre sleeve sts, k up 10 sts
up second side of left sleeve, patt across
centre front sts, k up 10 sts down first side of
right sleeve, k centre sleeve sts, k up 9 sts up
second side of right sleeve, k centre back sts.
143 sts.
**Next row** P1, *patt 34, p2, [k2, p4] 5 times,
k2, p3; rep from ★ once more.
**Next row** ★ K2, C2F, [k4, C2F] 5 times, k3,
patt 34; rep from ★ once more, k1.

Patt a further 13 rows as set.
**Next row** K2, [k2 tog, k4] to last 3 sts, k2
tog, k1. 119 sts.
Beg with a p row, work 9 rows in st st. Cast
off loosely.

**TO MAKE UP**
Wash garment according to the instructions
given on ball band. Join neckband seam,
reversing seam on st st section. Sew saddles
to shoulders. Sew on remainder of sleeves in
place. Join side and sleeve seams.

# Denim Fisherman Shirt page 14

## MATERIALS
13(15: 17: 19) 50g balls Rowan Denim.
Pair each of 3¼mm (No 10/US 3),
3¾mm (No 9/US 4) and 4mm (No
8/US 6) knitting needles.
Cable needle.

## TENSION
20 sts and 28 rows to 10cm/4in square
over st st on 4mm (No 8/US 6) needles.

## ABBREVIATIONS
**C2B** = sl next st onto cable needle and
leave at back of work, k1, then k1 tbl
from cable needle;
**C2F** = sl next st onto cable needle and
leave at front of work, k1 tbl, then k1
from cable needle;
**Cr2L** = sl next st onto cable needle
and leave at front of work, p1, then k1
from cable needle;
**Cr2R** = sl next st onto cable needle
and leave at back of work, k1, then p1
from cable needle;
**mb** = [k1, p1, k1, p1, k1] all in next st,
turn, p5, turn, k5, turn, p2 tog, p1, p2
tog tbl, turn, k3 tog.
Also see page 42.

## PANEL A
Worked over 9 sts.
**1st row (right side)** P2, Cr2R, k1 tbl,
Cr2L, p2.
**2nd row** K2, p1, [k1, p1] twice, k2.
**3rd row** P1, C2B, p1, k1 tbl, p1, C2F, p1.
**4th row** K1, p2, k1, p1, k1, p2, k1.
**5th row** Cr2R, k1 tbl, [p1, k1 tbl] twice,
Cr2L.
**6th row** P1, [k1, p1] 4 times.
**7th row** Cr2L, k1 tbl, [p1, k1 tbl] twice,
Cr2R.
**8th row** As 4th row.
**9th row** P1, Cr2L, p1, k1 tbl, p1, Cr2R, p1.
**10th row** As 2nd row.
**11th row** P2, Cr2L, k1 tbl, Cr2R, p2.
**12th row** K3, p3, k3.
**13th row** P3, sl next 2 sts onto cable needle
and leave at back of work, k1, then k1 tbl,
k1 from cable needle, p3.
**14th row** K3, p3, k3.
These 14 rows form patt.

## PANEL B
Worked over 9 sts.
**1st row (right side)** Sl next st onto cable
needle and leave at back of work, k1 tbl,
then k1 from cable needle, p7.
**2nd row** K6, Cr2L, p1.
**3rd row** K1 tbl, p1, C2F, p5.
**4th row** K4, Cr2L, p1, k1, p1.
**5th row** [K1 tbl, p1] twice, C2F, p3.
**6th row** K2, Cr2L, [p1, k1] twice, p1.
**7th row** [K1 tbl, p1] 3 times, C2F, p1.
**8th row** Cr2L, [p1, k1] 3 times, p1.
**9th row** [K1 tbl, p1] 4 times, k1 tbl.
**10th row** P1, [k1, p1] 3 times, Cr2L.
**11th row** P1, Cr2L, [p1, k1 tbl] 3 times.
**12th row** P1, [k1, p1] twice, Cr2L, k2.
**13th row** P3, Cr2L, [p1, k1 tbl] twice.
**14th row** P1, k1, p1, Cr2L, k4.
**15th row** P5, Cr2L, p1, k1 tbl.

## MEASUREMENTS

| To fit age | 3-5 | 6-7 | 7-8 | 9-10 | years |
|---|---|---|---|---|---|
| Actual chest | 96 | 104 | 116 | 124 | cm |
| measurement | 38 | 41 | 45½ | 49 | in |
| Length | 44 | 48 | 53 | 58 | cm |
| | 17½ | 19 | 21 | 23 | in |
| Sleeve seam | 26 | 32 | 36 | 40 | cm |
| | 10¼ | 12½ | 14¼ | 15¾ | in |

**16th row** P1, Cr2L, k6.
**17th row** P7, sl next st onto cable needle
and leave at front of work, k1, then k1 tbl
from cable needle.
**18th row** P1, Cr2R, k6.
**19th row** P5, C2B, p1, k1 tbl.
**20th row** P1, k1, p1, Cr2R, k4.
**21st row** P3, C2B, [p1, k1 tbl] twice.
**22nd row** P1, [k1, p1] twice, Cr2R, k2.
**23rd row** P1, C2B, [p1, k1 tbl] 3 times.
**24th row** P1, [k1, p1] 3 times, Cr2R.
**25th row** K1 tbl, [p1, k1 tbl] 4 times.
**26th row** Cr2R, [p1, k1] 3 times, p1.
**27th row** [K1 tbl, p1] 3 times, Cr2R, p1.
**28th row** K2, Cr2R, [p1, k1] twice, p1.
**29th row** [K1 tbl, p1] twice, Cr2R, p3.
**30th row** K4, Cr2R, p1, k1, p1.
**31st row** K1 tbl, p1, Cr2R, p5.
**32nd row** K6, Cr2R, p1.
These 32 rows form patt.

## PANEL C
Rep of 11 sts.
**1st row (right side)** ★ P3, Cr2R, k1,
Cr2L, p3; rep from ★.
**2nd row** *K3, p1, [k1, p1] twice, k3; rep
from ★.
**3rd row** ★ P2, Cr2R, k1, p1, k1, Cr2L, p2;
rep from ★.
**4th row** ★ K2, p1, [k1, p1] 3 times, k2; rep
from ★.
**5th row** ★ P1, Cr2R, k1, [p1, k1] twice,
Cr2L, p1; rep from ★.
**6th row** ★ K1, [p1, k1] 5 times; rep from ★.
**7th row** ★ Cr2R, k1, [p1, k1] 3 times,
Cr2L; rep from ★.
**8th row** ★ P1, [k1, p1] 5 times; rep from ★.
**9th row** ★ Cr2L, p1, [k1, p1] 3 times,
Cr2R; rep from ★.
**10th row** As 6th row.
**11th row** ★ P1, Cr2L, p1, [k1, p1] twice,
Cr2R, p1; rep from ★.

**12th row** As 4th row.
**13th row** ★ P2, Cr2L, p1, k1, p1, Cr2R, p2; rep from ★.
**14th row** As 2nd row.
**15th row** ★ P3, Cr2L, p1, Cr2R, p3; rep from ★.
**16th row** ★ K4, p1, k1, p1, k4; rep from ★.
**17th row** P4, ★ sl next 2 sts onto cable needle and leave at back of work, k1, then p1, k1 from cable needle★★, p4, pick up loop lying between st just worked and next st and work into back, front, back and front of the loop, then pass 2nd, 3rd, and 4th st over 1st st, p next st, then pass bobble st over the p st, p3★★★; rep from ★ to ★★★ to last 7 sts, rep from ★ to ★★, p4.
**18th row** As 16th row.
These 18 rows form patt.

## BACK

With 3¾mm (No 9/US 4) needles cast on 113(125: 137: 149) sts.
**1st row (right side)** P1, k3, ★p2, Cr2R, k1, Cr2L, p2, k3; rep from ★ to last st, p1.
**2nd row** K1, p3, ★ k2, p1, [k1, p1] twice, k2, p3; rep from ★ to last st, k1.
**3rd row** P1, k3, ★p1, Cr2R, p1, k1, p1, Cr2L, p1, k3; rep from ★ to last st, p1.
**4th row** K1, p3, ★, k1, p1, [k2, p1] twice, k1, p3; rep from ★ to last st, k1.
**5th row** P1, k3, ★ Cr2R, p2, k1, p2, Cr2L, k3; rep from ★ to last st, p1.
**6th row** K1, p3, ★ k4, p1, k4, p3; rep from ★ to last st, k1.
These 6 rows form welt patt. Rep last 6 rows 10(11: 12: 13) times more, dec one st at centre on 2nd and 4th sizes only. 113(124: 137: 148) sts.
Change to 4mm (No 8/US 6) needles.
**1st row (right side)** P1, [k3, welt patt 9 sts] 0(0: 1: 1) time, k3, work 1st row of panel A, k3, work 1st row of panel B, k3, welt patt 9 sts, k3, work 1st row of panel C across next 33(44: 33: 44) sts, k3, welt patt 9 sts, k3, work 17th row of panel B, k3, work 1st row of panel A, k3, [welt patt 9 sts, k3] 0(0: 1: 1) time, p1.
**2nd row** K1, [p3, welt patt 9 sts] 0(0: 1: 1) time, p3, work 2nd row of panel A, p3, work 18th row of panel B, p3, welt patt 9 sts, p3, work 2nd row of panel C across next 33(44: 33: 44) sts, p3, welt patt 9, p3, work 2nd row of panel B, p3, work 2nd row of panel A, p3, [welt patt 9, p3] 0(0: 1: 1) time, k1.
**3rd row** P1, [k1, mb, k1, welt patt 9 sts] 0(0: 1: 1) time, k1, mb, k1, work 3rd row of panel A, k1, mb, k1, work 3rd row of panel B, k1, mb, k1, welt patt 9 sts, k1, mb, k1, work 3rd row of panel C across next 33(44: 33: 44) sts, k1, mb, k1, welt patt 9 sts, k1, mb, k1, work 19th row of panel B, k1, mb, k1, work 3rd row of panel A, k1, mb, k1, [welt patt 9 sts, k1, mb, k1] 0(0: 1: 1) time, p1.
**4th row** K1, [p3, welt patt 9 sts] 0(0: 1: 1) time, p3, work 4th row of panel A, p3, work 20th row of panel B, p3, welt patt 9 sts, p3, work 4th row of panel C across next 33(44: 33: 44) sts, p3, welt patt 9 sts, p3, work 4th row of panel B, p3, work 4th row of panel A, p3, [welt patt 9 sts, p3] 0(0: 1: 1) time, k1.
**5th row** P1, [k3, welt patt 9 sts] 0(0: 1: 1) time, k3, work 5th row of panel A, k3, work 5th row of panel B, k3, welt patt 9 sts, k3, work 5th row of panel C across next 33(44: 33: 44) sts, k3, welt patt 9 sts, k3, work 21st row of panel B, k3, work 5th row of panel A, k3, [welt patt 9 sts, k3] 0(0: 1: 1) time, p1.
**6th row** K1, [p3, welt patt 9 sts] 0(0: 1: 1) time, p3, work 6th row of panel A, p3, work 22nd row of panel B, p3, welt patt 9 sts, p3, work 6th row of panel C across next 33(44: 33: 44) sts, p3, welt patt 9 sts, p3, work 6th row of panel B, p3, work 6th row of panel A, p3, [welt patt 9 sts, p3] 0(0: 1: 1) time, k1.
These 6 rows set position of panels and form bobble patt between panels. Cont in patt until Back measures 50(54: 60:66)cm/20 (21½: 24: 26¼)in from beg, ending with a wrong side row.

### Shape Neck

**Next row** Patt 43(48: 54: 59), turn.
Work on this set of sts only. Keeping patt correct, cast off 3 sts at beg of next row and foll alt row.

### Shape Shoulder

Cast off 12(14: 16: 18) sts at beg of next row and foll alt row. Work 1 row. Cast off rem 13(14: 16: 17) sts.
With right side facing, slip centre 27(28: 29: 30) sts onto a holder, rejoin yarn to rem sts, patt to end. Patt 1 row. Complete to match first side.

## FRONT

Work as given for Back until Front measures 46(50: 55: 61)cm/18¼(19¾: 22: 24¼)in from beg, ending with a wrong side row.

### Shape Neck

**Next row** Patt 45(50: 56: 61), turn.
Work on this set of sts only. Dec one st at neck edge on next 8 rows. 37(42: 48: 53) sts.
Cont straight until Front matches Back to shoulder shaping, ending at side edge.

### Shape Shoulder

Cast off 12(14: 16: 18) sts at beg of next row and foll alt row. Work 1 row. Cast off rem 13(14: 16: 17) sts.
With right side facing, slip centre 23(24: 25: 26) sts onto a holder, rejoin yarn to rem sts, patt to end. Complete to match first side.

## SLEEVES

With 3¼mm (No 10/US 3) needles cast on 57(59: 61: 63) sts.
**1st row (right side)** K0(1: 2: 3), p2, Cr2R, k1, Cr2L, p2, ★ k3, p2, Cr2R, k1, Cr2L, p2; rep from ★ to last 0(1: 2: 3) sts, k0(1: 2: 3).
**2nd row** P0(1: 2: 3), k2, p1, [k1, p1] twice, k2, ★p3, k2, p1, [k1, p1] twice, k2; rep from ★ to last 0(1: 2: 3) sts, p0(1: 2: 3).
These 2 rows set welt patt. Patt a further 16 rows.
Change to 4mm (No 8/US 6) needles.
**1st row (right side)** K0(1: 2: 3), welt patt 9 sts, k3, work 1st row of panel C across next 33 sts, k3, welt patt 9 sts, k0(1: 2: 3).
**2nd row** P0(1: 2: 3), welt patt 9 sts, p3, work 2nd row of panel C across next 33 sts, p3, welt patt 9, p0(1: 2: 3).
These 2 rows set position of panels. Cont in patt, inc one st at each end of next row and every foll 4th(5th: 5th: 6th) row until there are 85(89: 93: 97) sts, working inc sts into bobble patt then into moss st (k the p sts and p the k sts). Cont straight until Sleeve measures 30(37: 42: 47)cm/11¾(14½: 16½: 18½)in from beg, ending with a wrong side row. Cast off.

## NECKBAND

Join right shoulder seam.
With 3¼mm (No 10/US 3) needles and right side facing, k up 14(14: 17: 17) sts down left front neck, k centre front sts, k up 14(14: 17: 17) sts up right front neck, k up 8 sts down right back neck, k centre back sts, k up 8 sts up left back neck. 94(96: 104: 106) sts. Beg with a p row, work 15 rows in st st. Cast off loosely.

## TO MAKE UP

Wash garment according to the instructions given on ball band. Join left shoulder and neckband seam, reversing seam on last 6 rows of neckband. Sew on sleeves, placing centre of sleeves to shoulder seams. Join side and sleeve seams.

**Denim Fisherman Shirt**

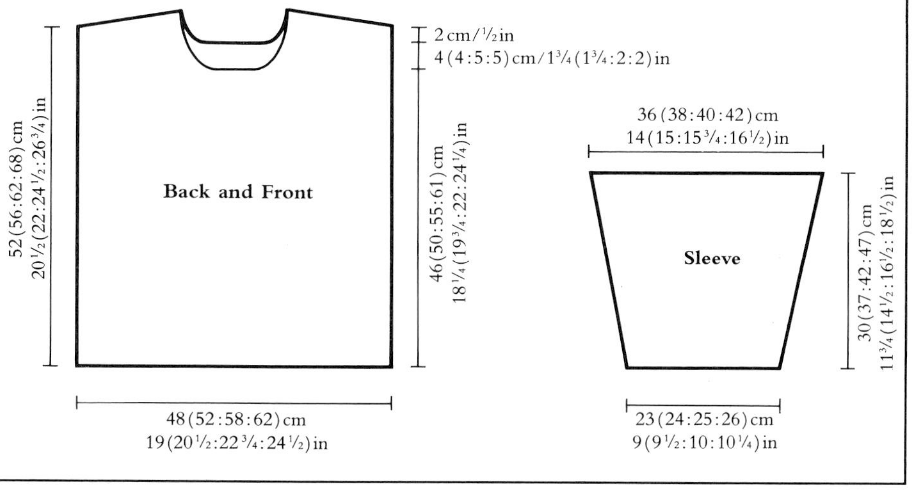

2 cm/½in
4(4:5:5)cm/1¾(1¾:2:2)in
52(56:62:68) cm
20½(22:24½:26¾)in
Back and Front
46(50:55:61) cm
18¼(19¾:22:24¼)in
48(52:58:62) cm
19(20½:22¾:24½)in
36(38:40:42)cm
14(15:15¾:16½)in
Sleeve
30(37:42:47)cm
11¾(14½:16½:18½)in
23(24:25:26) cm
9(9½:10:10¼)in

# Ribbed Sweater with Stripes

## MATERIALS

8(9: 11: 12: 14) 50g balls of Rowan DK Handknit Cotton in main colour (A). 2 balls of same in contrast colour (B). Pair each of 3¼mm (No 10/US 3) and 4mm (No 8/US 6) knitting needles.

## TENSION

21 sts and 30 rows to 10cm/4in square over pattern on 4mm (No 8/US 6) needles.

## ABBREVIATIONS

See page 42

## BACK

With 3¼mm (No 10/US 3) needles and A, cast on 88(93: 98: 108: 118) sts.
**1st row (right side)** K3, [p2, k3] to end.
**2nd row** P.
These 2 rows form patt. Work a further 2cm/¾in in patt.
Change to 4mm (No 8/US 6) needles.
Cont in patt until Back measures 14(16: 18: 20: 22)cm/5½(6¼: 7¼: 8: 8¾)in from beg, ending with a right side row. Change to B and patt 4 rows. Change to A and patt 4 rows. Change to B and patt 20(20: 22: 22: 22)

rows. Cont in A only until Back measures 46(49: 53: 57: 60)cm/18( 19¼: 21: 22½: 23½)in from beg, ending with a wrong side row.
**Shape Shoulders**
Cast off 15(15: 17: 19: 21) sts at beg of next 2 rows and 14(16: 16: 19: 21) sts at beg of foll 2 rows. Leave rem 30(31: 32: 32: 34) sts on a holder.

## FRONT

Work as given for Back until Front is 12(14: 16: 16: 18) rows less than Back to shoulder shaping, ending with a wrong side row.
**Shape Neck**
**Next row** Patt 37(39: 41: 46: 50), turn. Work on this set of sts only. Keeping patt correct, dec one st at neck edge on every row until 29(31: 33: 38: 42) sts rem. Patt 3(5: 7: 7: 9) rows straight.
**Shape Shoulder**
Cast off 15(15: 17: 19: 21) sts at beg of next row. Patt 1 row. Cast off rem 14(16: 16: 19: 21) sts.
With right side facing, slip centre 14(15: 16: 16: 18) sts onto a holder, rejoin yarn to rem sts and patt to end. Complete to match first side, but working 1 row more before shaping shoulder.

## SLEEVES

With 3¼mm (No 10/US 3) needles and A, cast on 43(43: 48: 48: 53) sts. Work 2cm/¾in in patt as given for Back.
Change to 4mm (No 8/US 6) needles. Work 7 rows in patt, inc one st at each end of 3rd row and foll 4th row. Change to B and patt 4 rows, inc one st at each end of 4th row. Change to A and patt 4 rows, inc one st at each end of 4th row. Change to B and patt 4 rows, inc one st at each end of 4th row.
Cont in A only, inc one st at each end of every foll 4th row until there are 75(83: 88: 94: 97) sts. Cont straight until Sleeve measures 28(31: 35: 38: 41)cm/11(12 ¼: 13¾ : 15: 16)in from beg, ending with a wrong side row. Cast off.

## NECKBAND

Join right shoulder seam.
With 3¼mm (No 10/US 3) needles, A, and right side facing, k up 19(18: 21: 21: 25) sts down left front neck, patt centre front sts, k up 18(17: 21: 21: 24) sts up right front neck, patt back neck sts dec one st at end on 1st and 5th sizes only. 80(81: 90: 90: 100) sts.
1st rib row P3(2: 0: 0: 0), [k2, p3] to last 2(4: 0: 0: 0) sts, k2(2: 0: 0: 0), p0(2: 0: 0: 0).
2nd rib row K0(2: 0: 0: 0), p2(2: 0: 0: 0), [k3, p2] to last 3(2: 0: 0: 0) sts, k3(2: 0: 0: 0).
Rep last 2 rows 4(4: 5: 5: 6) times more, then work 1st row again. Working k for p and p for k on next row (thus reversing fabric), rib 11(11: 13: 13: 15) rows. Cast off loosely in rib.

## TO MAKE UP

Join left shoulder and neckband seam, reversing seam on reversed part of neckband. Sew on sleeves, placing centre of sleeves to shoulder seams. Join side and sleeve

## MEASUREMENTS

| To fit age | 3-4 | 4-6 | 6-8 | 8-9 | 9-10 | years |
|---|---|---|---|---|---|---|
| Actual chest | 84 | 88 | 93 | 102 | 112 | cm |
| measurement | 33 | 34½ | 36½ | 40 | 44 | in |
| Length | 46 | 49 | 53 | 57 | 60 | cm |
| | 18 | 19¼ | 21 | 22½ | 23½ | in |
| Sleeve seam | 28 | 31 | 35 | 38 | 41 | cm |
| | 11 | 12¼ | 13¾ | 15 | 16 | in |

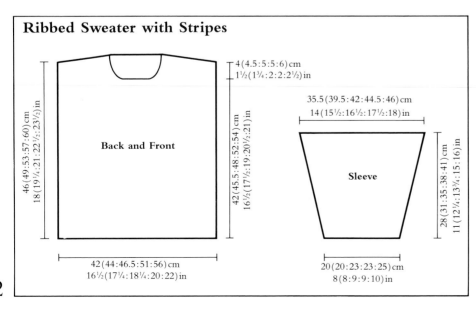

### Ribbed Sweater with Stripes

Back and Front

46(49:53:57:60)cm
18(19¼:21:22½:23½)in

42(45.5:48:52:54)cm
16½(17¾:19:20½:21)in

42(44:46.5:51:56)cm
16½(17¼:18¼:20:22)in

Sleeve

4(4.5:5:5:6)cm
1½(1¾:2:2:2½)in

35.5(39.5:42:44.5:46)cm
14(15½:16½:17½:18)in

28(31:35:38:41)cm
11(12¼:13¾:15:16)in

20(20:23:23:25)cm
8(8:9:9:10)in

# Stocking-stitch Sweater with Collar page 16

## MATERIALS
5(5: 6: 7: 7) 50g balls of Rowan True
4 ply Botany.
Pair each of 2¾mm (No 12/US 2) and
3¼mm (No 10/US 3) knitting needles.
Set of four 2¾mm (No 12/US 2)
double pointed knitting needles.

## TENSION
28 sts and 36 rows to 10cm/4in square
over st st on 3¼mm (No 10/US 3)
needles.

## ABBREVIATIONS
See page 42.

## BACK
With 2¾mm (No 12/US 2) needles cast on
98(114: 126: 140: 154) sts.
K 7 rows.
Change to 3¼mm (No 10/US 3) needles.
**Next row (right side)** K.
**Next row** K5, p to last 5 sts, k5.
Rep last 2 rows 3 times more. Beg with a k
row, work in st st until Back measures
38(45: 50: 55: 60)cm/15(17¾: 19¾: 21¾:
23¾)in from beg, ending with a p row.
**Shape Shoulders**
Cast off 14(17: 20: 23: 26) sts at beg of next
2 rows and 14(18: 20: 23: 26) sts at beg of

foll 2 rows. Leave rem 42(44: 46: 48: 50) sts
on a holder.

## FRONT
Work as given for Back until Front measures
34(40: 45: 49: 53)cm/13¼(15¾: 17¾:
19¼: 21)in from beg, ending with a p row.
**Shape Neck**
**Next row** K35(43: 48: 55: 62), turn.
Work on this set of sts only. Dec one st at
neck edge on every row until 28(35: 40: 46:
52) sts rem. Cont straight until Front
matches Back to shoulder shaping, ending at
side edge.
**Shape Shoulder**
Cast off 14(17: 20: 23: 26) sts at beg of next
row. Work 1 row. Cast off rem 14(18: 20: 23:
26) sts.
With right side facing, slip centre 28(28: 30:
30: 30) sts onto a holder, rejoin yarn to rem
sts and k to end. Complete as given for first
side.

## SLEEVES
With 2¾mm (No 12/US 2) needles cast on
54(54: 58: 62: 66) sts.
**1st rib row (right side)** K2, [p2, k2] to end.
**2nd row** P2, [k2, p2] to end.
Rep last 2 rows until cuff measures
5cm/2in, ending with a wrong side row and
inc 4(8: 8: 8: 8) sts evenly across last row.
58(62: 66: 70: 74) sts.
Change to 3¼mm (No 10/US 3) needles.
Beg with a k row, work in st st inc one st at
each end of 3rd row and every foll 4th row
until there are 84(96: 104: 112: 124) sts.
Cont straight until Sleeve measures 23(27:
30: 35: 40)cm/9(10: 11¾: 13¾: 15¾)in from
beg, ending with a p row. Cast off.

## COLLAR
Join shoulder seams.
With right side facing, slip first 14(14: 15:
15: 15) sts from centre front holder onto
spare needle, using set of four 2¾mm
(No 12/US 2) double pointed needles, k
rem 14(14: 15: 15: 15) sts, k up 20(22: 22:
24: 26) sts up right front neck, k back neck
sts, k up 20(22: 22: 24: 26) sts down left
front neck, then k sts fom spare needle.
110(116: 120: 126: 132) sts. Work 10(10: 12:
14: 14) rounds of k1, p1 rib.
Work forwards and backwards as follows:
**Next row** K80(84: 87: 91: 95), turn.
**Next row** K50(52: 54: 56: 58), turn.
**Next row** K54(56: 58: 60: 62), turn.
**Next row** K58(60: 62: 64: 66), turn.
Cont in this way, working 4 sts more at end
of foll 6 rows.
**Next row** K to end.
Cont in garter st (every row k) for a further
4(5: 5: 6)cm/1½(2: 2: 2½: 2½:) in. Cast
off loosely.

## TO MAKE UP
Sew on sleeves, placing centre of sleeves to
shoulder seams. Beg at top of side edge
borders, join side and sleeve seams.

## MEASUREMENTS

| To fit age | 1-2 | 3-4 | 4-6 | 6-8 | 8-10 | years |
|---|---|---|---|---|---|---|
| Actual chest | 70 | 81 | 90 | 100 | 110 | cm |
| measurement | 27½ | 32 | 35½ | 39½ | 43 | in |
| Length | 38 | 45 | 50 | 55 | 60 | cm |
| | 15 | 17¾ | 19¾ | 21¾ | 21¾ | in |
| Sleeve seam | 23 | 27 | 30 | 35 | 40 | cm |
| | 9 | 10½ | 11¾ | 13¾ | 15¾ | in |

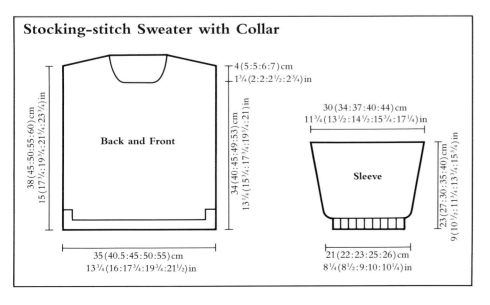

**Stocking-stitch Sweater with Collar**

Back and Front

38(45:50:55:60)cm
15(17¾:19¾:21¾:23¾)in

4(5:5:6:7)cm
1¾(2:2:2½:2¾)in

34(40:45:49:53)cm
13¼(15¾:17¾:19¼:21)in

35(40.5:45:50:55)cm
13¾(16:17¾:19¾:21½)in

Sleeve

30(34:37:40:44)cm
11¾(13½:14½:15¾:17¼)in

23(27:30:35:40)cm
9(10½:11¾:13¾:15¾)in

21(22:23:25:26)cm
8¼(8½:9:10:10¼)in

# Lace-edged Cardigan page 17

## MATERIALS
9(10: 11) 50g balls of Rowan
Cotton Glace.
Pair each of 3mm (No 11/US 2) and
3¾mm (No 9/US 4) knitting needles.
4(4: 5) buttons.
Cable needle.

## MEASUREMENTS

| To fit age | 4-6 | 6-8 | 8-10 | years |
|---|---|---|---|---|
| Actual chest | 86 | 94 | 103 | cm |
| measurement | 33¾ | 36¾ | 40¾ | in |
| Length | 35 | 38 | 43 | cm |
| | 13¾ | 15 | 17 | in |
| Sleeve seam | 30 | 32 | 38 | cm |
| | 12 | 12¾ | 15 | in |

## TENSION
24 sts and 30 rows to 10cm/4in square
over double moss stitch on 3¾mm
(No 9/US 4) needles.

## ABBREVIATIONS
**C2B** = sl next st onto cable needle and
leave at back of work, k1, then k1 from
cable needle;
**C2F** = sl next st onto cable needle and
leave at front of work, k1, then k 1 from
cable needle;
**C4B** = sl next 2 sts onto cable needle
and leave at back of work, k2, then k2
from cable needle;
**C4F** = sl next st onto cable needle and
leave at front of work, k2, then k2 from
cable needle;
**Cr2L** = sl next st onto cable needle and
leave at front of work, p1, then k1 from
cable needle;
**Cr2R** = sl next st onto cable needle
and leave at back of work, k1, then p1
from cable needle;
**Cr3L** = sl next 2 sts onto cable needle
and leave at front of work, p1, then k2
from cable needle;
**Cr3R** = sl next st onto cable needle
and leave at back of work, k2, then p1
from cable needle;
**MB** = [k1, p1, k1, p1] all in next st,
turn, p4, turn, k4, then pass 2nd, 3rd and
4th st over first st.
Also see page 42.

## PANEL A
Worked over 9 sts.
**1st row (right side)** P1, Cr3L, p5.
**2nd row** K5, p2, k2.
**3rd row** P1, k1, Cr3L, p4.
**4th row** K4, p2, k1, p1, k1.
**5th row** P2, k1, Cr3L, p3.
**6th row** K3, p2, k1, p1, k2.
**7th row** [P1, k1] twice, Cr3L, p2.
**8th row** K2, p2, k1, [p1, k1] twice.
**9th row** P2, k1, p1, k1, Cr3L, p1.
**10th row** K1, p2, [k1, p1] twice, k2.
**11th row** P1, [k1, p1] twice, Cr3R, p1.
**12th row** As 8th row.
**13th row** P2, k1, p1, Cr3R, p2.
**14th row** As 6th row.
**15th row** P1, k1, p1, Cr3R, p3.
**16th row** As 4th row.
**17th row** P2, Cr3R, p4.
**18th row** As 2nd row.
**19th row** P1, Cr3R, p5.
**20th row** K6, p2, k1.
These 20 rows form patt.

## PANEL B
Worked over 16 sts.
**1st row (right side)** ★ P6, C2B ★★, C2F,
p6 ★★★.
**2nd row** ★ K5, Cr2L, p1 ★★, p1, Cr2R, k5
★★★.
**3rd row** ★ P4, Cr2R, C2B ★★, C2F, Cr2L,
p4 ★★★.
**4th row** ★ K3, Cr2L, k1, p2 ★★, p2, k1,
Cr2R, k3 ★★★.
**5th row** ★ P2, Cr2R, p1, Cr2R, k1 ★★, k1,
Cr2L, p1, Cr2L, p2 ★★★.
**6th row** ★ [K2, p1] twice, k1, p1 ★★, p1, k1,
[p1, k2] twice ★★★.
**7th row** ★ P2, mb, p1, Cr2R, p1, k1 ★★, k1,
p1, Cr2L, p1, mb, p2 ★★★.
**8th row** ★ K4, p1, k2, p1 ★★, p1, k2, p1, k4
★★★.
**9th row** ★P4, mb, p2, k1 ★★, k1, p2, mb, p4
★★★.
**10th row** ★K7, p1 ★★, p1, k7 ★★★.
These 10 rows form patt.

## PANEL C
Worked over 9 sts.
**1st row (right side)** P5, Cr3R, p1.
**2nd row** K2, p2, k5.
**3rd row** P4, Cr3R, k1, p1.
**4th row** K1, p1, k1, p2, k4.
**5th row** P3, Cr3R, k1, p2.
**6th row** K2, p1, k1, p2, k3.
**7th row** P2, Cr3R, [k1, p1] twice.
**8th row** K1, [p1, k1] twice, p2, k2.
**9th row** P1, Cr3R, k1, p1, k1, p2.
**10th row** K2, [p1, k1] twice, p2, k1.
**11th row** P1, Cr3L, [p1, k1] twice, p1.
**12th row** As 8th row.
**13th row** P2, Cr3L, p1, k1, p2.
**14th row** As 6th row.
**15th row** P3, Cr3L, p1, k1, p1.
**16th row** As 4th row.
**17th row** P4, Cr3L, p2.
**18th row** As 2nd row.
**19th row** P5, Cr3L, p1.
**20th row** K1, p2, k6.
These 20 rows form patt.

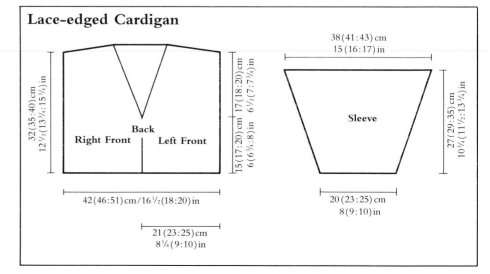

**Lace-edged Cardigan**

Back — Right Front — Left Front
32(35:40) cm 12½(13¾:15¾) in
15(17:20) cm 6(6¾:8) in
17(18:20) cm 6½(7:7¾) in
42(46:51) cm/16½(18:20) in
21(23:25) cm 8¼(9:10) in

Sleeve
38(41:43) cm 15(16:17) in
27(29:35) cm 10¾(11½:13¾) in
20(23:25) cm 8(9:10) in

## BACK

With 3¾mm (No 9/US 4) needles cast on 120(128: 140) sts.

**1st row (right side)** [K1, p1] 1(3: 6) times, [k4, work 1st row of panel A, k4, work 1st row of panel B from * to ***] twice, k4, work 1st row of panel C, k4, work 1st row of panel B from * to ***, k4, work 1st row of panel C, k4, [p1, k1] 1(3: 6) times.

**2nd row** [P1, k1] 1(3: 6) times, [p4, work 2nd row of panel C, p4, work 2nd row of panel B from * to ***] twice, p4, work 2nd row of panel A, p4, work 2nd row of panel B from * to ***, p4, work 2nd row of panel A, p4, [k1, p1] 1(3: 6) times.

**3rd row** [P1, k1] 1(3: 6) times, [C4F, work 3rd row of panel A, C4B, work 3rd row of panel B from * to ***] twice, C4F, work 3rd row of panel C, C4B, work 3rd row of panel B from * to ***, C4F, work 3rd row of panel C, C4B, [k1, p1] 1(3: 6) times.

**4th row** [K1, p1] 1(3: 6) times, [p4, work 4th row of panel C, p4, work 4th row of panel B from * to ***] twice, p4, work 4th row of panel A, p4, work 4th row of panel B from * to ***, p4, work 4th row of panel A, p4, [p1, k1] 1(3: 6) times.

These 4 rows set position of panels and form cable patt between panels and double moss st at side edges. Cont in patt until Back measures 32(35: 40)cm/12 1/2(13¾: 15¾)in from beg, ending with a wrong side row.

### Shape Shoulders

Cast off 20(21: 24) sts at beg of next 2 rows and 20(22: 24) sts at beg of foll 2 rows. Cast off rem 40(42: 44) sts, working [k2 tog] twice over each cable and at centre of panel B and k2 tog at centre of panel A and C.

## LEFT FRONT

With 3¾mm (No 9/US 4) needles cast on 61(65: 71) sts.

**1st row (right side)** [K1, p1] 1(3: 6) times, k4, work 1st row of panel A, k4, work 1st row of panel B from * to ***, k4, work 1st row of panel A, k4, work 1st row of panel B from * to **, k1.

**2nd row** P1, work 2nd row of panel B from ** to ***, p4, work 2nd row of panel A, p4, work 2nd row of panel B from * to ***, p4, work 2nd row of panel A, p4, [k1, p1] 1(3: 6) times.

**3rd row** [P1, k1] 1(3: 6) times, C4F, work 3rd row of panel A, C4B, work 3rd row of panel B from * to ***, C4F, work 3rd row of panel A, C4B, work 3rd row of panel B from * to **, k1.

**4th row** P1, work 4th row of panel B from ** to ***, p4, work 4th row of panel A, p4, work 4th row of panel B from * to ***, p4, work 4th row of panel A, p4, [p1, k1] 1(3: 6) times.

These 4 rows set position of panels and form cable patt between panels and double moss st at side edge. Cont in patt until Front measures 15(17: 20)cm/6(6¾: 8)in from beg, ending with a wrong side row.

### Shape Neck

Keeping patt correct, dec one st at front edge on next row and every foll alt row until 40(43: 48) sts rem. Cont straight until Front matches Back to shoulder shaping, ending at side edge.

### Shape Shoulder

Cast off 20(21: 24) sts at beg of next row. Work 1 row. Cast off rem 20(22: 24) sts.

## RIGHT FRONT

With 3¾mm (No 9/US 4) needles cast on 61(65: 71) sts.

**1st row (right side)** K1, work 1st row of panel B from ** to ***, k4, work 1st row of panel C, k4, work 1st row of panel B from * to ***, k4, work 1st row of panel C, k4, [p1, k1] 1(3: 6) times.

**2nd row** [P1, k1] 1(3: 6) times, p4, work 2nd row of panel C, p4, work 2nd row of panel B from * to ***, p4, work 2nd row of panel C, p4, work 2nd row of panel B from * to **, p1.

**3rd row** K1, work 3rd row of panel B from ** to ***, C4F, work 3rd row of panel C, C4B, work 3rd row of panel B from * to ***, C4F, work 3rd row of panel C, C4B, [k1, p1] 1(3: 6) times.

**4th row** [K1, p1] 1(3: 6) times, p4, work 4th row of panel C, p4, work 4th row of panel B from * to ***, p4, work 4th row of panel C, p4, work 4th row of panel B from * to **, p1.

These 4 rows set position of panels and form cable patt between panels and double moss st at side edge. Complete as given for Left Front.

## SLEEVES

With 3¾mm (No 9/US 4) needles cast on 58(66: 70) sts.

**1st row (right side)** [K1, p1] 2(4: 5) times, k4, work 1st row of panel A, k4, work 1st row of panel B from * to ***, k4, work 1st row of panel C, k4, [p1, k1] 2(4: 5) times.

**2nd row** [P1, k1] 2(4: 5) times, p4, work 2nd row of panel C, p4, work 2nd row of panel B from * to ***, p4, work 2nd row of panel A, p4, [k1, p1] 2(4: 5) times.

**3rd row** [P1, k1] 2(4: 5) times, C4B, work 3rd row of panel A, C4F, work 3rd row of panel B from * to ***, C4B, work 3rd row of panel C, C4F, [k1, p1] 2(4: 5) times.

**4th row** [K1, p1] 2(4: 5) times, p4, work 4th row of panel C, p4, work 4th row of panel B from * to ***, p4, work 4th row of panel A, p4, [p1, k1] 2(4: 5).

These 4 rows set position of panels and form cable patt betwenn panels and double moss st at side edges. Cont in patt, inc one st at each end of next row and every foll 3rd(3rd: 4th) row until there are 100(108: 112) sts, working inc sts into double moss st. Cont straight until Sleeve measures 27(29: 35)cm/10¾(11½: 13¾)in from beg, ending with a wrong side row. Cast off.

## BUTTON BAND

With 3mm (No 11/US 2) needles cast on 8 sts.

Work in p1, k1 rib until band, when slightly stretched fits along straight front edge of Left Front. Cast off in rib. Sew band in place.

Mark band to indicate positions of 4(4: 5) buttons: first one 2cm/½in up from lower edge, last one 1cm/¼in below top edge and rem 2(2: 3) evenly spaced between.

## BUTTONHOLE BAND

With 3mm (No 11/US 2) needles cast on 8 sts. Work in k1, p1 rib until first marker on Button Band is reached.

**Buttonhole row (right side)** Rib 2, k2 tog, yf, rib to end.

Complete as given for Button Band, making buttonholes at markers as before.

## WELT EDGING

With 3mm (No 11/US 2) needles cast on 4 sts.

K 1 row.

**1st row** K2, yf, k2.

**2nd row and 2 foll alt row (right side)** Sl1, k to end.

**3rd row** K3, yf, k2.

**5th row** K2, yf, k2 tog, yf, k2.

**7th row** K3, yf, k2 tog, yf, k2.

**8th row** Cast off 4, k to end.

These 8 rows form patt. Cont in patt until edging, when slightly stretched, fits along lower edges of Fronts and Back, ending with 8th row of patt. Cast off.

## SLEEVE EDGINGS (make 2)

Work as given for Welt Edging until edging fits along lower edge of sleeve, ending with 8th row of patt. Cast off.

## COLLAR

Join shoulder seams.

Work as given for Welt Edging, inc one st at beg of 3rd row of patt and 12 foll 4th rows, working inc sts as k. Cont straight until shaped edge of Collar, when slightly stretched, fits up shaped edge of Right Front to centre of back neck, ending with 8th row of patt. Work other half of Collar to match, working dec instead of inc and ending with 8th row of patt. Cast off.

## TO MAKE UP

Sew sleeve edings in place. Sew on sleeves, placing centre of sleeves to shoulder seams. Join side and sleeve seams. Sew on welt edging and collar in place, catching cast on and off sts of collar to centre of front bands. Sew on buttons.

## MATERIALS

7(8: 9) 50g balls of Rowan Cotton Glace in Cream (A).
1 ball of same in each of Dark Green, Purple, Brown, Lilac and Light Green.
Pair each of 3¼mm (No 10/US 3) and 3¾mm (No 9/US 4) knitting needles.
6 buttons.

## MEASUREMENTS

| To fit age | 4–6 | 6–8 | 8–10 years | |
|---|---|---|---|---|
| Actual chest | 80 | 89 | 96 | cm |
| measurement | 31½ | 35 | 38 | in |
| Length | 35 | 38 | 43 | cm |
| | 13¾ | 15 | 17 | in |
| Sleeve seam | 32 | 35 | 38 | cm |
| | 12½ | 13¾ | 15 | in |

## TENSION

23 sts and 32 rows to 10cm/4in square over st st on 3¾mm (No 9/US 4) needles.

## ABBREVIATIONS

See page 42.

## NOTES

Read charts from right to left on right side (k) rows and from left to right on wrong side (p) rows. When working flower motifs, use separate lengths of contrast colours on each coloured area and twist yarns together on wrong side at joins to avoid holes.

## BACK

With 3¼mm (No 10/US 3) needles and A, cast on 93(103: 111) sts.
**1st row** K1, [p1, k1] to end.
This row forms moss st. Moss st 7 rows more.
Change to 3¾mm (No 9/US 4) needles.
Beg with a k row, work 6 rows in st st.
**Next row (right side)** K11(15: 17)A, k 1st row of chart 1, k33(35: 39)A, k 1st row of chart 1, with A, k to end.
**Next row** P11(15: 17)A, p 2nd row of chart 1, p33(35: 39)A, p 2nd row of chart 1, with A, p to end.
Work a further 11 rows as set. With A and beg with a p row, work 19 rows in st st.
**1st row** K19(24: 28)A, k 1st row of chart 2, k21A, k 1st row of chart 2, with A, k to end.
**2nd row** P19(24: 28)A, p 2nd row of chart 2, p21A, p 2nd row of chart 2, with A, p to end.
Work a further 7 rows as set. With A, work 12 rows.
**22nd row** P6(10: 12)A, p 1st row of chart 2, [p15(16: 18)A, p 1st row of chart 2] twice, with A, p to end.
**23rd row** K6(10: 12)A, k 2nd row of chart 2, [k15(16: 18)A, k 2nd row of chart 2] twice, with A, k to end.
Work a further 7 rows as set. With A, work 12 rows.
The last 42 rows form patt. Cont in patt until Back measures 35(38: 43)cm/13¾(15: 17)in from beg, ending with a wrong side row.
### Shape Shoulders
Cast off 14(15: 17) sts at beg of next 2 rows and 14(16: 17) sts at beg of foll 2 rows.
Leave rem 37(41: 43) sts on a holder.

## POCKET LININGS (make 2)

With 3¾mm (No 9/US 4) needles and A, cast on 27 sts.
Beg with a k row, work 26 rows in st st.
Leave these sts on a holder.

## LEFT FRONT

With 3¼mm (No 10/US 3) needles and A, cast on 43(47: 51) sts.
Work 8 rows in moss st as given for Back, inc one st at centre of last row on 2nd and 3rd sizes only. 43(48: 52) sts.
Change to 3¾mm (No 9/US 4) needles.
Beg with a k row, work 6 rows in st st.
**Next row (right side)** K11(15: 17)A, k 1st row of chart 1, with A, k to end.
**Next row** P13(14: 16)A, p 2nd row of chart 1, with A, p to end.
Work a further 11 rows as set. Cont in A only. Beg with a p row, work 5 rows in st st.
**Next row** K8(12: 14), p1, [k1, p1] 12 times, k to end.
**Next row** P9(10: 12), k1, [p1, k1] 13 times, p to end.
Rep last 2 rows once more, then work 1st of the 2 rows again.
**Next row** P9(10: 12), cast off in moss st next 27 sts, p to end.
**Place Pocket**
**Next row** K7(11: 13), k across sts of pocket lining, k to end.
Work a further 7 rows in st st.
**1st row** K19(24: 28)A, k 1st row of chart 2, k7A.
**2nd row** P7A, p 2nd row of chart 2, with A, p to end.
Work a further 7 rows as set. With A, work 12 rows.
**22nd row** 20(21: 23)A, p 1st row of chart 2, with A, p to end.
**23rd row** K6(10: 12)A, k 2nd row of chart 2, with A, k to end.
Work a further 7 rows as set. With A, work 12 rows.
The last 42 rows form patt. Cont in patt until Front measures 29(31: 35)cm/11½ (12 ¼: 14)in from beg, ending with a right side row.

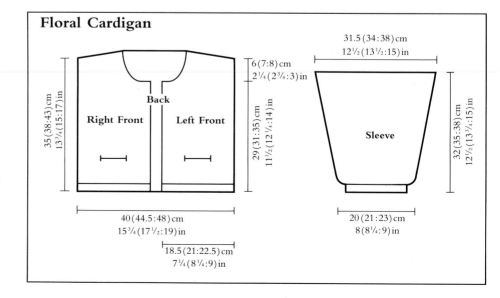

**Floral Cardigan**

Back
Right Front
Left Front

35(38:43)cm
13¾(15:17)in

29(31:35)cm
11½(12¼:14)in

6(7:8)cm
2¼(2¾:3)in

40(44.5:48)cm
15¾(17½:19)in

18.5(21:22.5)cm
7¼(8¼:9)in

Sleeve

31.5(34:38)cm
12½(13½:15)in

32(35:38)cm
12½(13¾:15)in

20(21:23)cm
8(8¼:9)in

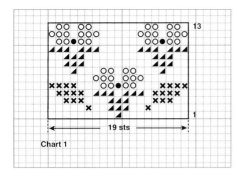

Chart 1
19 sts

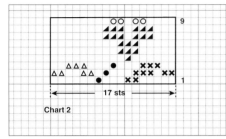

Chart 2
17 sts

**KEY**

| | |
|---|---|
| ☐ | Cream (A) |
| ✖ | Dark Green |
| ◢ | Purple |
| ● | Brown |
| ○ | Lilac |
| ▲ | Light Green |

**Shape Neck**
Keeping patt correct, cast off 4 sts at beg of next row and foll alt row. Dec one st at neck edge on next 5 rows, then on every alt row until 28(31: 34) sts rem. Cont straight until Front matches Back to shoulder shaping, ending with a wrong side row.

**Shape Shoulder**
Cast off 14(15: 17) sts at beg of next row. Work 1 row. Cast off rem 14(16: 17) sts.

**RIGHT FRONT**
With 3¼mm (No 10/US 3) needles and A, cast on 43(47: 51) sts.
Work 8 rows in moss st as given for Back, inc one st at centre of last row on 2nd and 3rd sizes only. 43(48: 52) sts.
Change to 3¾mm (No 9/US 4) needles.
Beg with a k row, work 6 rows in st st.
**Next row (right side)** K13(14: 16)A, k 1st row of chart 1, with A, k to end.
**Next row** P11(15: 17)A, p 2nd row of chart 1, with A, p to end.
Work a further 11 rows as set. Cont in A only. Beg with a p row, work 5 rows in st st.
**Next row** K10(11: 13), p1, [k1, p1] 12 times, k to end.
**Next row** P7(11: 13), k1, [p1, k1] 13 times, p to end.
Rep last 2 rows once more, then work 1st of the 2 rows again.
**Next row** P7(11: 13), cast off in moss st next 27 sts, p to end.

**Place Pocket**
Next row K9(10: 12), k across sts of pocket lining, k to end.
Work a further 7 rows in st st.

**1st row** K7A, k 1st row of chart 2, with A, k to end.
**2nd row** P19(24: 28)A, p 2nd row of chart 2, p7A.
Work a further 7 rows as set. With A, work 12 rows.
**22nd row** P6(10: 12)A, p 1st row of chart 2, with A, p to end.
**23rd row** K20(21: 23)A, k 2nd row of chart 2, with A, k to end.
Work a further 7 rows as set. With A, work 12 rows. The last 42 rows form patt. Complete to match Left Front, reversing shapings.

**SLEEVES**
With 3¼mm (No 10/US 3) needles and A, cast on 43(45: 47) sts.
Work 8 rows in moss st as given for Back, inc 4 sts evenly across last row. 47(49: 51) sts.
Change to 3¾mm (No 9/US 4) needles.
Beg with a k row, work 6 rows in st st, inc one st at each end of 5th row. 49(51: 53) sts.
**Next row (right side)** K15(16: 17)A, k 1st row of chart 1, with A, k to end.
**Next row** P15(16: 17)A, p 2nd row of chart 1, with A, p to end.
Work a further 11 rows as set, inc one st at each end of 3rd row and foll 6th row. With A, work 19 rows in st st, inc one st at each end of 4th row and 2 foll 6th rows. 59(61: 63) sts.
**Next row** K2(3: 4)A, k 1st row of chart 2, k21A, k 1st row of chart 2, with A, k to end.
Next row P2(3: 4)A, p 2nd row of chart 2, p21A, p 2nd row of chart 2, with A, p to end.
Work a further 7 rows as set, inc one st at each end of 1st row and foll 6th row. With A, work 12 rows, inc one st at each end of 2 foll 6th rows. 67(69: 71) sts.
**Next row** P25(26: 27)A, p 1st row of chart 2, with A, p to end.
**Next row** K25(26: 27)A, k 2nd row of chart 2, with A, k to end.
Work a further 7 rows as set, inc one st at each end of 4th row. With A, work 12 rows, inc one st at each end of 3rd row and foll 6th row. 73(75: 77) sts. The last 42 rows set patt.

**2nd and 3rd sizes only**
Cont in patt, inc one st at each end of 2nd row and (1: 2) foll 6th rows. (79: 83) sts.

**All sizes**
Cont straight in patt until Sleeve measures 32(35: 38)cm/12½(13¾: 15)in from beg, ending with a wrong side row. Cast off.

**NECKBAND**
Join shoulder seams.
With 3¼mm (No 10/US 3) needles, A and right side facing, k up 23(26: 29) sts up right front neck, k back neck sts dec 4 sts evenly, k up 23(26: 29) sts down left front neck. 79(89: 97) sts. Moss st 8 rows. Cast off in moss st.

**BUTTON BAND**
With 3¼mm (No 10/US 3) needles and A, cast on 8 sts.
**1st row** [K1, p1] to end.
**2nd row** [P1, k1] to end.
These 2 rows form moss st. Cont in moss st

until band, when slightly stretched, fits up Left Front to top of neckband. Cast off. Sew band in position. Mark band to indicate position of 6 buttons: first one 4 rows up from lower edge, last one 4 rows down from top edge and rem 4 evenly spaced between.

**BUTTONHOLE BAND**
Work as given for Button Band, but beg moss st with 2nd row and making buttonholes to match markers as follows:
**Buttonhole row** Moss st 2, p2 tog, yrn, moss st 4.

**TO MAKE UP**
Sew on sleeves, placing centre of sleeves to shoulder seams. Join side and sleeve seams. Catch down pocket linings. Sew on buttons.

# Moss-stitch Tunic with Hat page 18

## TUNIC

### BACK
With 4mm (No 8/US 6) needles cast on 67(73: 85: 95: 105: 115) sts.
**1st row** K1, [p1, k1] to end.
This row forms moss st. Cont in moss st until Back measures 33(38: 45: 50: 55: 60)cm/13(15: 17¾: 19¾: 21¾: 23¾)in from beg.

## MEASUREMENTS

| | TUNIC | | | | | | |
|---|---|---|---|---|---|---|---|
| To fit age | 1 | 1-2 | 3-4 | 4-6 | 6-8 | 8-10 | years |
| Actual chest | 64 | 69 | 80 | 90 | 100 | 109 | cm |
| measurement | 25 | 27 | 31½ | 35½ | 39½ | 43 | in |
| Length | 33 | 38 | 45 | 50 | 55 | 60 | cm |
| | 13 | 15 | 17¾ | 19¾ | 21¾ | 23¾ | in |
| Sleeve seam | | | | | | | |
| *(with cuff* | 20 | 23 | 28 | 32 | 38 | 40 | cm |
| *turned back)* | 8 | 9 | 11 | 12½ | 15 | 15¾ | in |
| | HAT | | | | | | |
| To fit age | 1-2 | 2-6 | years | | | | |

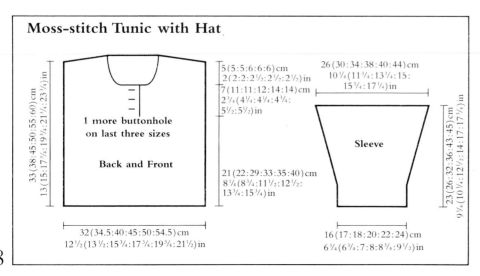

**Moss-stitch Tunic with Hat**

Back and Front — 1 more buttonhole on last three sizes
33(38:45:50:55:60)cm 13(15:17¾:19¾:21¼:23¾)in
32(34.5:40:45:50:54.5)cm 12½(13½:15¾:17¾:19¾:21½)in
5(5:5:6:6:6)cm 2(2:2:2½:2½:2½)in
7(11:11:12:14:14)cm 2¾(4¼:4¼:4¾:4¾)in / 5½:5½)in
21(22:29:33:35:40)cm 8¼(8¾:11½:12½:13¾:15¾)in

Sleeve
26(30:34:38:40:44)cm 10¼(11¾:13¼:15:15¾:17¼)in
23(26:32:36:43:45)cm 9¼(10¼:12½:14:17:17¾)in
16(17:18:20:22:24)cm 6¼(6¾:7:8:8¾:9½)in

### Shape Shoulders
Cast off 10(11: 14: 16: 18: 20) sts at beg of next 4 rows. Leave rem 27(29: 29: 31: 33: 35) sts on a holder.

### FRONT
Work as given for Back until Front measures 21(22: 29: 32: 35: 40)cm/8¼(8¾: 11½: 12½: 13¾: 15¾)in from beg.
**Divide for Opening**
**Next row** Patt 31(34: 40: 45: 50: 55), turn; leave rem 36(39: 45: 50: 55: 60) sts on a spare needle.
Cast on 5 sts at beg of next row for button band. Cont in patt on this set of 36(39: 45: 50: 55: 60) sts until Front measures 28(33: 40: 44: 49: 54)cm/11(13: 15¾: 17¼: 19¼: 21¼)in from beg, ending at inside edge.
### Shape Neck
**Next row** Cast off 3, patt 4 sts more, leave these 5 sts on a safety pin, patt to end.
Dec one st at neck edge on next 5(7: 7: 7: 9: 9) rows, then on every foll alt row until 20(22: 28: 32: 36: 40) sts rem. Cont straight until Front matches Back to shoulder shaping, ending at side edge.
### Shape Shoulder
Cast off 10(11: 14: 16: 18: 20) sts at beg of next row. Work 1 row. Cast off rem 10(11: 14: 16: 18: 20) sts.
Mark button band to indicate position of 3(3: 3: 4: 4: 4) buttons: first one 2(3: 3: 2: 4: 4)cm/¾(1¼: 1¼: ¾: 1½: 1½)in from cast on edge, last one 1cm/¼in below neck shaping and rem 1(1: 1: 2: 2: 2) evenly spaced between.
Rejoin yarn at inside edge to sts on a spare needle and patt to end. Patt a further 2(3: 3: 2: 4: 4)cm/ ¾(1¼: 1¼: ¾: 1½: 1½)in, ending at inside edge.
**Buttonhole row** Patt 2, p2 tog, yrn, patt to end.
Complete as given first side, making buttonholes at markers as before.

### SLEEVES
With 4mm (No 8/US 6) needles cast on 33(35: 39: 43: 47: 51) sts.
Work 3(3: 4: 4: 5: 5)cm/1¼(1¼: 1½: 1½: 2: 2)in in moss st as given for Back.
Change to 3¼mm (No 10/US 3) needles.
Cont in moss st for a further 3(3: 4: 4: 5: 5)cm/1¼(1¼: 1½: 1½: 2: 2)in.
Change to 4mm (No 8/US 6) needles.
Cont in moss st, inc one st at each end of next row and every foll 4th(4th: 4th: 5th: 5th: 5th) row until there are 55(63: 71: 79: 85: 93) sts, working inc sts into patt.
Cont straight until Sleeve measures 23(26: 32: 36: 43: 45)cm/9¼(10¼: 12½: 14: 17: 17¾)in from beg. Cast off.

### COLLAR
Join shoulder seams.
With 3¼mm (No 10/US 3) needles and right side facing, sl 5 sts on right side front safety pin onto needle, k up 11(12: 12: 15: 16: 17) sts up right front neck, moss st across back neck sts, k up 11(12: 12: 15: 16: 17) sts down left front neck, moss st 5 sts from left

58

side front safety pin. 59(63: 63: 71: 75: 79) sts. Moss st 1 row across all sts.
**Next 2 rows** Moss st to last 17(17: 17: 21: 21: 21) sts, turn.
**Next 2 rows** Moss st to last 14(14: 14: 17: 17: 17) sts, turn.
**Next 2 rows** Moss st to last 11(11: 11: 13: 13: 13) sts, turn.
**Next 2 rows** Moss st to last 8(8: 8: 9: 9: 9) sts, turn.
Cont in moss st across all sts, inc one st at each end of 5 foll 4th rows. Moss st 2 rows. Cast off in moss st.

## TO MAKE UP
Sew on sleeves, placing centre of sleeves to shoulder seams. Join side and sleeve seams. Catch down cast on edge of button band on wrong side. Sew on buttons.

## HAT

### EAR FLAPS (make 2)
With 4mm (No 8/US 6) needles cast on 9 sts.
**1st row** K1, [p1, k1] to end.
This row forms moss st. Cont in moss st, inc one st at each end of next row and 3(4) foll alt rows. 17(19) sts. Moss st 6(10) rows straight. Dec one st at each end of next row and foll alt row. Now inc one st at each end of 2nd row and 2 foll rows. 19(21) sts. Moss st 1 row. Leave these sts on a holder.

### MAIN PART
With 4mm (No 8/US 6) needles cast on 11(13), moss st across first ear flap, cast on 33(37), moss st across second ear flap, cast on 12(14). 94(104) sts.
Cont in moss st, work 29(33) rows.
**Shape Top**
**1st row** [Moss st 15(17), work 3 tog] 5 times, moss st 4.
Moss st 3 rows.
**5th row** [Moss st 13(15), work 3 tog] 5 times, moss st 4.
Moss st 3 rows.
**9th row** [Moss st 11(13), work 3 tog] 5 times, moss st 4.
Cont in this way, dec 10 sts as set on every foll 4th row until 34 sts rem. Work 1 row.
**Next row** [Moss st 7, work 3 tog, moss st 7] twice.
Work 1 row.
**Next row** [Moss st 6, work 3 tog, moss st 6] twice.
Work 1 row.
**Next row** [Moss st 5, work 3 tog, moss st 5] twice.
Cont in this way, dec 4 sts as set on every foll alt row until 6 sts rem. Work 1 row.
Break off yarn, thread end through rem sts, pull up and secure. Join back seam.

# Guernsey with Ribbed Yoke page 19

## MATERIALS
3(4: 5: 5: 6: 7) 50g balls of Rowan True 4 ply Botany.
Pair each of 3mm (No 11/US 2) and 3¼mm (No 10/US 3) knitting needles.
3 buttons for 1st and 2nd sizes only.

## TENSION
28 sts and 36 rows to 10cm/4in square over st st on 3¼mm (No 10/US 3) needles.

## ABBREVIATIONS
See page 42.

## BACK
With 3mm (No 11/US 2) needles cast on 88(98: 113: 128: 143: 158) sts.
K 9(9: 11: 11: 13: 13) rows.
Change to 3¼mm (No 10/US 3) needles. Beg with a k row, work in st st until Back measures 18(21: 25: 28: 31: 34)cm/7(8¼: 10: 11: 12¼: 13¼)in from beg, ending with a p row.
**Next row (right side)** K3, [p2, k3] to end.
**Next row** P.
The last 2 rows form yoke patt. Cont in yoke patt until Back measures 31(36: 43: 48: 53: 58)cm/12¼(14¼: 17: 18¾: 20¾: 22¾)in from beg, ending with a wrong side row.
**Shape Neck**
**Next row** Patt 31(35: 40: 48: 53: 59), turn.
Work on this set of sts only. Keeping patt correct, dec one st at neck edge on next

6(6: 6: 8: 8: 8) rows. Patt 1 row. Cast off rem 25(29: 34: 40: 45: 51) sts.
With right side facing, slip centre 26(28: 33: 32: 37: 40) sts onto a holder, rejoin yarn to rem sts, patt to end. Complete as given for first side.

## FRONT
Work as given for Back, until Front measures 29(34: 40: 45: 49: 54)cm/11½(13½: 15¾: 17½: 19¼: 21¼)in from beg, ending with a wrong side row.

## MEASUREMENTS

| To fit age | 1 | 2–3 | 4–5 | 6–7 | 8–9 | 9–10 | years |
|---|---|---|---|---|---|---|---|
| Actual chest | 62 | 70 | 80 | 91 | 102 | 112 | cm |
| measurement | 24½ | 27½ | 31½ | 36 | 40 | 44 | in |
| Length | 33 | 38 | 45 | 51 | 56 | 61 | cm |
| | 13 | 15 | 17¾ | 20 | 22 | 24 | in |
| Sleeve seam | 20 | 23 | 28 | 32 | 38 | 40 | cm |
| | 8 | 9 | 11 | 12½ | 15 | 15¾ | in |

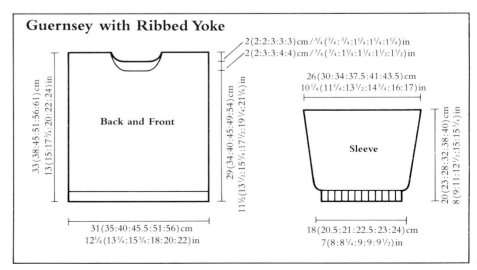

**Guernsey with Ribbed Yoke**

2(2:2:3:3:3)cm / ¾(¾:¾:1¼:1¼:1¼)in
2(2:3:3:4:4)cm / ¾(¾:1¼:1¼:1½:1½)in

**Back and Front**

33(38:45:51:56:61)cm
13(15:17¾:20:22:24)in

29(34:40:45:49:54)cm
11½(13½:15¾:17½:19¼:21¼)in

31(35:40:45.5:51:56)cm
12¼(13¾:15¾:18:20:22)in

26(30:34:37.5:41:43.5)cm
10¼(11¾:13½:14¾:16:17)in

**Sleeve**

20(23:28:32:38:40)cm
8(9:11:12½:15:15¾)in

18(20.5:21:22.5:23:24)cm
7(8:8¼:9:9:9½)in

**Shape Neck**

**Next row** Patt 35(39: 45: 51: 57: 64), turn. Work on this set of sts only. Dec one st at neck edge on every row until 25(29: 34: 40: 45: 51) sts rem. Cont straight until Front matches Back to cast off edge, ending with a wrong side row. Cast off.
With right side facing, slip centre 18(20: 23: 26: 29: 30) sts onto a holder, rejoin yarn to rem sts, patt to end. Complete as given for first side.

**SLEEVES**

With 3mm (No 11/US 2) needles cast on 50(54: 54: 58: 58: 62) sts.
**1st rib row (right side)** K2, [p2, k2] to end.
**2nd rib row** P2, [k2, p2] to end.
Rib a further 8(10: 12: 14: 16: 18) rows, inc 2(4: 5: 5: 7: 6) sts evenly across last row. 52(58: 59: 63: 65: 68) sts.
Change to 3¼mm (No 10/US 3) needles. Beg with a k row, work in st st, inc one st at each end of 5th row and every foll 4th row until there are 68(78: 83: 93: 103: 108) sts, ending with a p row.
Now work in yoke patt as given for Back, inc one st at each end of 4th row and every foll 6th(4th: 4th: 4th: 4th: 4th) row until there are 72(84: 95: 105: 115: 122) sts, working inc sts into patt. Cont straight until Sleeve measures 20(23: 28: 32: 38: 40)cm/8(9: 11: 12½: 15: 15¾)in from beg, ending with a wrong side row. Cast off.

**NECKBAND**

Join right shoulder seam.
With 3mm (No 11/US 2) needles and right side facing, k up 15(15: 17: 18: 20: 20) sts down left front neck, k centre front sts, k up 15(15: 17: 18: 20: 20) sts up right front neck, 8(8: 8: 10: 10: 10) sts down right back neck, k centre back sts, k up 8(8: 8: 10: 10: 10) sts up left back neck. 90(94: 106: 114: 126: 130) sts. Beg with a 2nd row, work 7(9: 11: 13: 13: 15) rows in rib as given for Sleeves. Beg with a k row, work 6(6: 8: 8: 10: 10) rows in st st. Cast off loosely.

**TO MAKE UP**

**1st and 2nd sizes only**
With 3mm (No 11/US 2) needles and right side facing, k up 31(36) sts along rib part of neckband and left back shoulder for button band. K 3 rows. Cast off.
With 3mm (No 11/US 2) needles and right side facing, k up 31(36) along left front shoulder and rib part of neckband for buttonhole band. K 1 row.
**Buttonhole row** K7(9), [yf, k2 tog, k8(9)] twice, yf, k2 tog, k2(3).
K 1 row. Cast off. Lap buttonhole band over button band and catch together row ends at side edge. Sew on sleeves, placing centre of sleeves to shoulders. Join sleeve seams, then side seams, leaving lower edging open. Sew on buttons.
**3rd, 4th, 5th and 6th sizes only**
Join left shoulder and neckband seam, reversing seam on last 5 rows of neckband. Sew on sleeves, placing centre of sleeves to shoulder seams. Join sleeve seams, then side seams, leaving lower edging open.

# Denim Wrap page 20

**MATERIALS**
18 50g balls of Rowan Denim.
Pair of 3¾mm (No 9/US 4) and 4½mm (No 7/US 7) knitting needles.
Cable needle.

**MEASUREMENTS**
Approximately 82.5cm x 130cm/32½ in x 51in after washing.

**TENSION**
19 sts and 28 rows to 10cm/4in square over moss st on 4½mm (No 7/US 7) needles before washing.

**ABBREVIATIONS**
**C3B** = sl next st onto cable needle and leave at back of work, k2, then k1 from cable needle;
**C3F** = sl next 2 sts onto cable needle and leave at front of work, k1, then k2 from cable needle;
**C6F** = sl next 3 sts onto cable needle and leave at front of work, k3, then k3 from cable needle;
**Cr2L** = sl next st onto cable needle and leave at front of work, p1, then k1 from cable needle;
**Cr2R** = sl next st onto cable needle and leave at back of work, k1, then p1 from cable needle;
**Cr3L** = sl next 2 sts onto cable needle and leave at front of work, p1, then k2 from cable needle;
**Cr3R** = sl next 2 sts onto cable needle and leave at back of work, k2, then p1 from cable needle.
Also see page 42

**PANEL A**
Worked over 8 sts.
**1st row (right side)** K6, p1, k1.
**2nd row** P2, k1, p5.
**3rd row** K4, [p1, k1] twice.
**4th row** P2, k1, p1, k1, p3.
**5th row** K2, [p1, k1] 3 times.
**6th row** P2, [k1, p1] 3 times.
**7th row** As 5th row.
**8th row** As 4th row.
**9th row** As 3rd row.
**10th row** As 2nd row.
These 10 rows form patt.

**PANEL B**
Worked over 18 sts.
**1st row (right side)** P5, k8, p5.
**2nd row** K5, p8, k5.
**3rd row** P4, Cr2R, k6, Cr2L, p4.
**4th row** K4, p1, k1, p6, k1, p1, k4.
**5th row** P3, Cr2R, p1, k6, p1, Cr2L, p3.
**6th row** K3, p1, k2, p6, k2, p1, k3.
**7th row** P2, Cr2R, p2, C6F, p2, Cr2L, p2.
**8th row** K2, p1, k3, p6, k3, p1, k2.
**9th row** P1, Cr2R, p3, k6, p3, Cr2L, p1.
**10th row** K1, p1, k4, p6, k4, p1, k1.

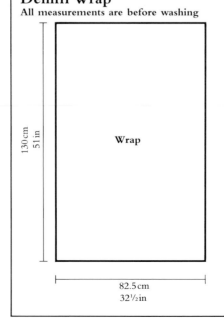

**Denim Wrap**
All measurements are before washing

130cm
51in

**Wrap**

82.5cm
32½in

**11th row** P1, Cr2L, p3, k6, p3, Cr2R, p1.
**12th row** As 8th row.
**13th row** P2, Cr2L, p2, C6F, p2, Cr2R, p2.
**14th row** As 6th row.
**15th row** P3, Cr2L, p1, k6, p1, Cr2R, p3.
**16th row** As 4th row.
**17th row** P4, Cr2L, k6, Cr2R, p4.
**18th row** K5, p8, k5.
Rows 3 to 18 form patt.

### PANEL C
Worked over 8 sts.
**1st row (right side)** K1, p1, k6.
**2nd row** P5, k1, p2.
**3rd row** [K1, p1] twice, k4.
**4th row** P3, k1, p1, k1, p2.
**5th row** [K1, p1] 3 times, k2.
**6th row** [P1, k1] 3 times, p2.
**7th row** As 5th row.
**8th row** As 4th row.
**9th row** As 3rd row.
**10th row** As 2nd row.
These 10 rows form patt.

### PANEL D
Worked over 14 sts.
**1st row (right side)** P3, k8, p3.
**2nd row** K3, p8, k3.

**3rd row** P4, C3B, Cr3L, p4.
**4th row** K4, p3, k1, p2, k4.
**5th row** P3, Cr3R, k1, p1, C3F, p3.
**6th row** K3, p2, [k1, p1] twice, p2, k3.
**7th row** P3, C3B, [p1, k1] twice, Cr3L, p2.
**8th row** K2, p3, [k1, p1] twice, k1, p2, k2.
**9th row** P1, Cr3R, [k1, p1] 3 times, C3F, p1.
**10th row** K1, p2, [k1, p1] 4 times, p2, k1.
**11th row** P1, Cr3L, [k1, p1] 3 times, Cr3R, p1.
**12th row** As 8th row.
**13th row** P2, Cr3L, [p1, k1] twice, Cr3R, p2.
**14th row** As 6th row.
**15th row** P3, Cr3L, k1, p1, Cr3R, p3.
**16th row** As 4th row.
**17th row** P4, Cr3L, Cr3R, p4.
**18th row** K5, p4, k5.
**19th row** P3, sl next 2 sts onto cable needle and leave at back of work, k2, then k2 from cable needle, sl next 2 sts onto cable needle and leave at front of work, k2, then k2 from cable needle, p3.
**20th row** K3, p8, k3.
**21st row** P3, k8, p3.
**22nd row** As 20th row.
**23rd and 24th rows** As 19th and 20th rows.
These 24 rows form patt.

### TO MAKE
With 3¾mm (No 9/US 4) needles cast on 171 sts.
**1st row** P1, [k1, p1] to end.
This row forms moss st. Moss st 4 rows more.
**Inc row** Moss st 17, *[inc in next st, moss 1] twice, [inc in next st, moss st 19] twice; rep from * twice more, [inc in next st, moss st 1] 3 times, moss st 16. 186 sts.
Change to 4½mm (No 7/US 7) needles.
**1st row (right side)** Moss st 4, [work 1st row of panels A, B, C and D] 3 times, work 1st row of panels A, B and C, moss st 4.
**2nd row** Moss st 4, [work 2nd row of panels C, B, A and D] 3 times, work 2nd row of panels C, B and A, moss st 4.
These 2 rows set position of panels. Patt 375 rows more.
**Dec row** Patt 17, *[work 2 tog, patt 1] twice, [work 2 tog, patt 19] twice; rep from * twice more, [work 2 tog, patt 1] 3 times, patt 16. 171 sts.
Change to 3¾mm (No 9/US 4) needles.
Work 6 rows in moss st across all sts. Cast off in moss st.

# Moss-stitch Beret page 20

### MATERIALS
1(2) 50g balls of Rowan Cotton Glace.
**1st size**
Pair each of 2¾mm (No 12/US 1) and 3¼mm (No 10/US 3) knitting needles.
**2nd size**
Pair each of 3mm (No 11/US 2) and 3¾mm (No 9/US 4) knitting needles.

### MEASUREMENTS

| To fit age | 1-2 | 3-6 | years |
| --- | --- | --- | --- |

### ABBREVIATIONS
See page 42.

### TO MAKE
With 2¾mm (No 12/US 1) needles for 1st size or 3mm (No 11/US 2) needles for 2nd size, cast on 96 sts.
Work 7 rows in k1, p1 rib.
**Inc row** Rib 3, m1, rib 3, [m1, rib 2, m1, rib 3] to end. 133 sts.
Change to 3¼mm (No 10/US 3) needles for 1st size and 3¾mm (No 9/US 4) needles.
**1st row** K1, [p1, k1] to end.
This row forms moss st patt. Cont in patt until work measures 9(11)cm/3½(4¼)in from beg.
**Shape Top**
**Dec row** [Patt 19, p3 tog] to last st, patt 1. Moss st 1 row.
**Dec row** [Patt 17, p3 tog] to last st, patt 1. Moss st 1 row.
**Dec row** [Patt 15, p3 tog] to last st, patt 1. Cont in this way, dec 12 sts as set on every alt row until 13 sts rem.
Break off yarn, thread end through rem sts, pull up and secure. Join back seam.

## MATERIALS

15(17: 19) 50g balls of Rowan DK Handknit Cotton.
Pair each of 3¼mm (No 10/US 3) and 4mm (No 8/US 6) knitting needles.
Cable needle.

## MEASUREMENTS

| To fit age | 4-7 | 7-9 | 9-10 years | |
| --- | --- | --- | --- | --- |
| Actual chest | 100 | 112 | 126 | cm |
| measurement | 39½ | 44 | 49½ | in |
| Length | 52 | 57 | 62 | cm |
| | 20½ | 22½ | 24½ | in |
| Sleeve seam | 35 | 37 | 39 | cm |
| | 13¾ | 14½ | 15½ | in |

## TENSION

20 sts and 28 rows to 10cm/4in square over st st on 4mm (No 8/US 6) needles.

## ABBREVIATIONS

**C4B** = sl next 2 sts onto cable needle and leave at back of work, k2, then k2 from cable needle;

**C4F** = sl next 2 sts onto cable needle and leave at front of work, k2, then k2 from cable needle;

**C2BK** = sl next st onto cable needle and leave at back of work, k1 tbl, then k1 tbl from cable needle;

**C2FK** = sl next st onto cable needle and leave at front of work, k1 tbl, then k1 tbl from cable needle;

**Cr2L** = sl next st onto cable needle and leave at front of work, p1, then k1 tbl from cable needle;

**Cr2R** = sl next st onto cable needle and leave at back of work, k1tbl, then p1 from cable needle;

**Cr3L** = sl next 2 sts onto cable needle and leave at front of work, p1, then k2 from cable needle;

**Cr3R** = sl next 2 sts onto cable needle and leave at back of work, k2, then p1 from cable needle;

**Tw2** =k into front of 2nd st on left hand needle, then k 1st st, sl both sts of needle tog.
Also see page 42.

## PANEL A
Worked over 20 sts.

**1st row (right side)** P6, C2BK, p1, Tw2, p1, C2FK, p6.
**2nd row** K6, p2, k1, p2 tbl, k1, p2, k6.
**3rd row** P5, Cr2R, k1 tbl, p1, Tw2, p1, k1 tbl, Cr2L, p5.
**4th row** K5, [p1, k1] twice, p2 tbl, [k1, p1] twice, k5.
**5th row** P4, Cr2R, C2BK, p1, Tw2, p1, C2FK, Cr2L, p4.
**6th row** K4, p1, k1, p2, k1, p2 tbl, k1, p2, k1, p1, k4.
**7th row** P3, [Cr2R] twice, k1 tbl, p1, Tw2, p1, k1 tbl, [Cr2L] twice, p3.
**8th row** K3, [p1, k1] 3 times, p2 tbl, [k1, p1] 3 times, k3.
**9th row** P2, [Cr2R] twice, C2BK, p1, Tw2, p1, C2FK, [Cr2L] twice, p2.
**10th row** K2, [p1, k1] twice, p2, k1, p2 tbl, k1, p2, [k1, p1] twice, k2.
**11th row** P1, [Cr2R] 3 times, k1 tbl, p1, Tw2, p1, k1 tbl, [Cr2L] 3 times, p1.

**12th row** [K1, p1] 4 times, k1, p2 tbl, k1, [p1, k1] 4 times.
**13th and 14th rows** As 9th and 10th rows.
**15th and 16th rows** As 7th and 8th rows.
**17th and 18th rows** As 5th and 6th rows.
**19th and 20th rows** As 3rd and 4th rows.
**21st and 22nd rows** As 1st and 2nd rows.
**23rd row** P7, k1 tbl, p1, Tw2, p1, k1 tbl, p7.
**24th row** K7, p1, k1, p2 tbl, k1, p1, k7.
**25th row** P9, Tw2, p9.
**26th row** K9, p2 tbl, k9.
**27th and 28th rows** As 25th and 26th rows.
These 28 rows form patt.

## PANEL B
Worked over 14 sts.

**1st row (right side)** P4, sl next st onto cable needle and leave at back of work, k2, then k1 from cable needle, sl next 2 sts onto cable needle and leave at front of work, k1, then k2 from cable needle, p4.
**2nd row** K4, p6, k4,
**3rd row** P3, Cr3R, Tw2, Cr3L, p3.
**4th row** K3, [p2, k1] 3 times, k2.
**5th row** P2, Cr3R, p1, Tw2, p1, Cr3L, p2.
**6th row** [K2, p2] 3 times, k2.
**7th row** P1, Cr3R, p2, Tw2, p2, Cr3L, p1.
**8th row** K1, [p2, k3] twice, p2, k1.
**9th row** P1, Cr3L, p2, Tw2, p2, Cr3R, p1.
**10th row** As 6th row.
**11th row** P2, Cr3L, p1, Tw2, p1, Cr3R, p2.
**12th row** As 4th row.
**13th row** P3, Cr3L, Tw2, Cr3R, p3.
**14th row** As 2nd row.
**15th row** P4, Cr3L, Cr3R, p4.
**16th row** K5, p4, k5.
**17th row** P5, k4, p5.
**18th row** K5, p4, k5.
These 18 rows form patt.

## PANEL C
Worked over 28 sts.

**1st row (right side)** [P1, k1 tbl] 7 times, [k1 tbl, p1] 7 times.
**2nd row** [K1, p1 tbl] 7 times, [p1 tbl, k1] 7 times.
**3rd row** [P1, k1 tbl] 4 times, [Cr2R] twice, C2BK, C2FK, [Cr2L] twice, [k1 tbl, p1] 4 times.

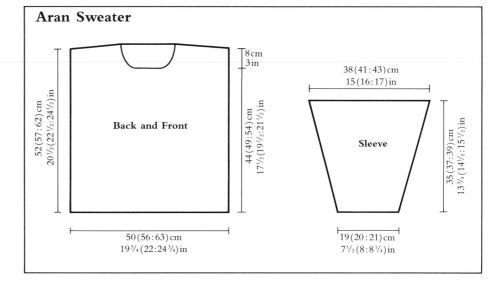

## Aran Sweater

Back and Front
52(57:62) cm
20½(22½:24½) in
44(49:54) cm
17½(19½:21½) in
8cm
3in

50(56:63) cm
19¾(22:24¾) in

Sleeve
38(41:43) cm
15(16:17) in
35(37:39) cm
13¾(14½:15½) in
19(20:21) cm
7½(8:8¼) in

**4th row** [K1, p1 tbl] 4 times, [p1 tbl, k1] twice, p4 tbl, [k1, p1 tbl] twice, [p1 tbl, k1] 4 times.

**5th row** P1, [k1 tbl, p1] 3 times, [Cr2R] 3 times, Tw2, [Cr2L] 3 times, [p1, k1 tbl] 3 times, p1.

**6th row** As 2nd row.

**7th row** [P1, k1 tbl] 3 times, [Cr2R] 3 times, p1, Tw2, p1, [Cr2L] 3 times, [k1 tbl, p1] 3 times.

**8th row** [K1, p1 tbl] 3 times, [p1 tbl, k1] 3 times, k1, p2 tbl, k1, [k1, p1 tbl] 3 times, [p1 tbl, k1] 3 times.

**9th row** [P1, k1 tbl] twice, p1, [Cr2R] 3 times, p2, Tw2, p2, [Cr2L] 3 times, p1, [k1 tbl, p1] twice.

**10th row** [K1, p1 tbl] 5 times, k3, p2 tbl, k3, [p1 tbl, k1] 5 times.

**11th row** [P1, k1 tbl] twice, [Cr2R] 3 times, p3, Tw2, p3, [Cr2L] 3 times, [k1 tbl, p1] twice.

**12th row** [K1, p1 tbl] twice, [p1 tbl, k1] 3 times, k3, p2 tbl, k3, [k1, p1 tbl] 3 times, [p1 tbl, k1] twice.

**13th row** P1, k1 tbl, p1, [Cr2R] 3 times, p4, Tw2, p4, [Cr2L] 3 times, p1, k1 tbl, p1.

**14th row** [K1, p1 tbl] 4 times, k5, p2 tbl, k5, [p1 tbl, k1] 4 times.

**15th row** P1, k1 tbl, [Cr2R] 3 times, p5, Tw2, p5, [Cr2L] 3 times, k1 tbl, p1.

**16th row** K1, p2 tbl, [k1, p1 tbl] twice, k6, p2 tbl, k6, [p1 tbl, k1] twice, p2 tbl, k1.

**17th row** P1, k1 tbl, [Cr2L] 3 times, p5, Tw2, p5, [Cr2R] 3 times, k1 tbl, p1.

**18th row** As 14th row.

**19th row** P1, k1 tbl, p1, C2FK, [Cr2L] twice, p4, Tw2, p4, [Cr2R] twice, C2BK, p1, k1 tbl, p1.

**20th row** As 12th row.

**21st row** [P1, k1 tbl] twice, [Cr2L] 3 times, p3, Tw2, p3, [Cr2R] 3 times, [k1 tbl, p1] twice.

**22nd row** As 10th row.

**23rd row** [P1, k1 tbl] twice, p1, C2FK, [Cr2L] twice, p2, Tw2, p2, [Cr2R] twice, C2BK, p1, [k1 tbl, p1] twice.

**24th row** As 8th row.

**25th row** [P1, k1 tbl] 3 times, [Cr2L] 3 times, p1, Tw2, p1, [Cr2R] 3 times, [k1 tbl, p1] 3 times.

**26th row** As 2nd row.

**27th row** [P1, k1 tbl] 3 times, p1, C2FK, [Cr2L] twice, Tw2, [Cr2R] twice, C2BK, p1, [k1 tbl, p1] 3 times.

**28th row** As 4th row.

**29th row** [P1, k1 tbl] 4 times, [Cr2L] 3 times, [Cr2R] 3 times, [k1 tbl, p1] 4 times.
Rows 2nd to 29th form patt.

## BACK
With 3¼mm (No 10/US 3) needles cast on 104(120: 136) sts.
Beg with a k row, work 5 rows in st st.
**Next row** P5(6: 7), ★m1, p3(4: 5), m1, p4; rep from ★ to last 1(2: 3) sts, p to end. 132(148: 164) sts.
Change to 4mm (No 8/US 6) needles.
**1st row (right side)** P2, [Tw2, p2] 1(3: 5) times, k4, work 1st row of panel A, k4, work 1st row of panel B, k4, work 1st row of panel C, k4, work 1st row of panel B, k4, work 1st row of panel A, k4, [p2, Tw2] 1(3: 5) times, p2.
**2nd row** K2, [p2 tbl, k2] 1(3: 5) times, p4, work 2nd row of panel A, p4, work 2nd row

of panel B, p4, work 2nd row of panel C, p4, work 2nd row of panel B, p4, work 2nd row of panel A, p4, [k2, p2 tbl] 1(3: 5) times, k2.
**3rd row** P2, [Tw2, p2] 1(3: 5) times, C4F, work 3rd row of panel A, C4F, work 3rd row of panel B, C4F, work 3rd row of panel C, C4B, work 3rd row of panel B, C4B, work 3rd row of panel A, C4B, [p2, Tw2] 1(3: 5) times, p2.
**4th row** K2, [p2 tbl, k2] 1(3: 5) times, p4, work 4th row of panel A, p4, work 4th row of panel B, p4, work 4th row of panel C, p4, work 4th row of panel B, p4, work 4th row of panel A, p4, [k2, p2 tbl] 1(3: 5) times, k2.
These 4 rows set position of panels, form cable patt between panels and twisted rib patt at side edges. Cont in patt until Back measures approximately 52(57: 62)cm/20½ (22½: 24½)in from beg, ending with 28th(14th: 28th) row of panel C patt.
**Shape Shoulders**
Cast off 22(25: 29) sts at beg of next 2 rows and 21(25: 28) sts at beg of foll 2 rows.
Leave rem 46(48: 50) sts on a holder.

## FRONT
Work as given for Back until Front measures approximately 44(49: 54) cm/17½(19½: 21½)in from beg, ending with 6th(20th:6th) row of panel C patt.
**Shape Neck**
**Next row** Patt 50(58: 66), turn.
Work on this set of sts only. Keeping patt correct, dec one st at neck edge on next 4 rows then on every alt row until 43(50: 57) sts rem. Cont straight until Front matches Back to shoulder shaping, ending at side edge.
**Shape Shoulder**
Cast off 22(25: 29) sts at beg of next row. Work 1 row. Cast off rem 21(25: 28) sts. With right side facing, slip centre 32 sts onto a holder, rejoin yarn to rem sts and patt to end. Complete to match first side.

## SLEEVES
With 3¼mm (No 10/US 3) needles cast on 47(49: 51) sts.
Beg with a k row, work 5 rows in st st.
**Next row** P7(8: 9), [m1, p8] 5 times, p0(1: 2). 52(54: 56) sts.
Change to 4mm (No 8/US 6) needles.
**1st row (right side)** P0(1: 2), [Tw2, p2] twice, k4, work 1st row of panel C, k4, [p2, Tw2] twice, p0(1: 2).
**2nd row** K0(1: 2), [p2 tbl, k2] twice, p4, work 2nd row of panel C, p4, [k2, p2 tbl] twice, k0(1: 2).
**3rd row** P0(1: 2), [Tw2, p2] twice, C4F, work 3rd row of panel C, C4B, [p2, Tw2] twice, p0(1: 2).
**4th row** K0(1: 2), [p2 tbl, k2] twice, p4, work 4th row of panel C, p4, [k2, p2 tbl] twice, k0(1: 2).
These 4 rows set position of panel, form cable patt at each side of panel and twisted rib patt at side edges. Cont in patt, inc one st at each end of next row and 13 foll 3rd rows, then on every foll 4th row until 98(104: 108) sts, working inc sts into twisted rib patt. Cont straight until Sleeve measures 35(37: 39)cm/13¾(14½: 15½)in from beg, ending with a wrong side row. Cast off.

## NECKBAND
Join right shoulder seam.
**1st and 3rd sizes only**
With 3¼mm (No 10/US 3) needles and right side facing, k up 25 sts down left front neck, work across centre front sts as follows: [p1, k1 tbl] 3 times, p3 tog, [k1 tbl, p1] 3 times, k2 tog tbl, [p1, k1 tbl] 3 times, p3 tog, [k1 tbl, p1] 3 times, k up 24 sts up righ front neck, work across back neck sts as follows: [k1 tbl, p1] 1(2) times, k2 tog tbl, p1, k1 tbl, p2 tog, [k1 tbl, p1] 4 times, k2 tog tbl, [p1, k1 tbl] twice, p2 tog, [k1 tbl, p1] twice, k2 tog tbl, [p1, k1 tbl] 4 times, p2 tog, [k1 tbl, p1] 3(4) times. 116(120) sts.
**2nd size only**
With 3¼mm (No 10/US 3) needles and right side facing, k up 25 sts down left front neck, work across centre front sts as follows: p1, [k1 tbl, p1] twice, k2 tog tbl, [p1, k1 tbl] 4 times, p2 tog, [k1 tbl, p1] 4 times, k2 tog tbl, [p1, k1 tbl] twice, p1, k up 24 sts up right front neck, work across back neck sts as follows: [k1 tbl, p2 tog] 3 times, [k1 tbl, p1] 5 times, k3 tog tbl, p1, k2 tog tbl, p1, k3 tog tbl, [p1, k1 tbl] 5 times, p2 tog, k1 tbl, p1, k1 tbl, p2 tog, k1 tbl, p1. 116 sts.
**All sizes**
**1st rib row** [K1, p1 tbl] to end.
**2nd rib row** [K1 tbl, p1] to end.
Rib a further 3 rows. Beg with a k row, work 6 rows in st st. Cast off loosely.

## TO MAKE UP
Join left shoulder and neckband seam, reversing seam on st st section of neckband. Sew in sleeves, placing centre of sleeves to shoulder seams. Join side and sleeve seams, reversing seams on first and last 6 rows.

## MATERIALS

15(17) 50g balls of Rowan DK Handknit Cotton.
Pair each of 3¼mm (No 10/US 3) and 4mm (No 8/US 6) knitting needles.
Cable needle.

## MEASUREMENTS

| To fit age | 4-6 | 8-10 | years |
|---|---|---|---|
| Actual chest | 92 | 116 | cm |
| measurement | 36 | 45½ | in |
| Length | 50 | 58 | cm |
| | 19 ¾ | 23 | in |
| Sleeve seam | 32 | 37 | cm |
| | 12 ½ | 14½ | in |

## TENSION

20 sts and 28 rows to 10cm/4in square over st st on 4mm (No 8/US 6) needles.

## ABBREVIATIONS

See page 42.

## PANEL A

Worked over 16 sts.
**1st row (right side)** P2, k2, p2, k4, p2, k2, p2.
**2nd row** K2, p2, k2, p4, k2, p2, k2.
**3rd to 8th rows** Rep 1st and 2nd rows 3 times.
**9th row** P2, sl next 4 sts onto cable needle and leave at back of work, k2, then p2, k2 from cable needle, sl next 2 sts onto cable needle and leave at front of work, k2, p2, then k2 from cable needle, p2.
**10th row** As 2nd row.
**11th to 14th rows** Rep 1st and 2nd rows twice.
**15th row** As 1st row.
**16th to 20th rows** K16.
These 20 rows form patt.

## PANEL B

Worked over 14 sts.
**1st row (right side)** K4, [p1, k4] twice.
**2nd row** K5, p4, k5.
**3rd row** K4, p1, sl next 2 sts onto cable needle and leave at front of work, k2, then k2 from cable needle, p1, k4.
**4th row** As 2nd row.
**5th and 6th rows** As 1st and 2nd rows.
These 6 rows form patt.

## BACK

With 3¼mm (No 10/US 3) needles cast on 92(116) sts.
**1st rib row (right side)** P1, k2, [p2, k2] to last st, p1.
**2nd rib row** K1, p2, [k2, p2] to last st, k1.
Rib a further 5 rows.
**Inc row** Rib 2, [m1, rib 7, m1, rib 2, m1, rib 7, m1, rib 3, m1, rib 2, m1, rib 3] to last 18 sts, [m1, rib, 7, m1, rib, 2] twice. 114(144) sts.
Change to 4mm (No 8/US 6) needles.
**1st row (right side)** K4, work 1st row of panel A, [work 1st row of panel B, then panel A] to last 4 sts, k4.
The last row sets position of panels and forms garter st at side edges. Cont in patt until Back measures 50(58)cm/19 3/4(23)in from beg, ending with a wrong side row.

## Shape Shoulders

Cast off 20(26) sts at beg of next 2 rows and 20(27) sts at beg of foll 2 rows. Leave rem 34(38) sts on a holder.

## FRONT

Work as given for Back until Front measures 39(47)cm/15¼(18½)in from beg, ending with a wrong side row.
### Shape Neck
**Next row** Patt 55(70), turn.
Work on this set of sts only. Dec one st at neck edge on next 4 rows then on every foll alt row until 40(53) sts rem. Cont straight until Front matches Back to shoulder shaping, ending at side edge.
### Shape Shoulder
Cast off 20(26) sts at beg of next row. Work 1 row. Cast off rem 20(27) sts.
With right side facing, slip centre 4 sts onto a safety pin, rejoin yarn to rem sts, patt to end. Complete to match first side.

## SLEEVES

With 3¼mm (No 10/US 3) needles cast on 44 sts.
Work 15 rows in rib as given for Back welt.
**Inc row** [Rib 2, m1, rib 7, m1] twice, rib 3, m1, rib 2, m1, rib 3, [m1, rib 7, m1, rib 2] twice. 54 sts.
Change to 4mm (No 8/US 6) needles.
**1st row (right side)** K4, work 1st row of panel A, then panel B and panel A, k4.
This row set position of panels. Cont in patt, inc one st at each end of 10 foll alt rows, working inc sts into panel B patt. 74 sts. Now inc one st at each end of every foll 4th row until there are 98(106) sts, working inc sts into garter st. Cont straight until Sleeve measures 32(37)cm/12½(14½)in from beg, ending with a wrong side row.
Cast off.

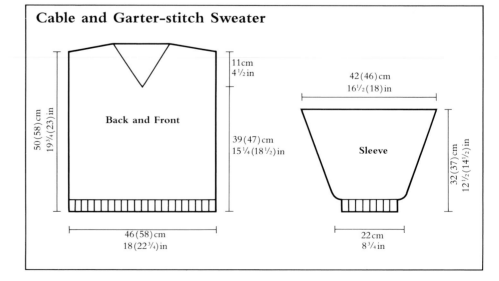

**Cable and Garter-stitch Sweater**

Back and Front

11cm 4½in

50(58)cm 19¾(23)in

39(47)cm 15¼(18½)in

46(58)cm 18(22¾)in

42(46)cm 16½(18)in

Sleeve

32(37)cm 12½(14½)in

22cm 8¾in

## NECKBAND

Join right shoulder seam.
With 3¼mm (No 10/US 3) needles and right side facing, k up 34 sts down left front neck, [k2 tog] twice across sts on safety pin (mark these 2 sts), k up 34 sts up right front neck, k back neck sts. 104(108) sts.
**1st rib row** P2, [k2, p2] to 2 sts before marked sts, k2 tog tbl, p2, k2 tog, [p2, k2] to end.

**2nd rib row** P2, [k2, p2] to 3 sts before marked sts, k1, k2 tog tbl, k2, k2 tog, k1, [p2, k2] to end.
**3rd row** Rib to 2 sts before marked sts, p2 tog tbl, p2, p2 tog, rib to end.
**4th row** Rib to 2 sts before marked sts, p2 tog tbl, k2, p2 tog, rib to end.
**5th row** Rib to 2 sts before marked st, k2 tog tbl, p2, k2 tog, rib to end.
Cast off in rib, dec one st at each side of marked sts as before.

## TO MAKE UP

Join left shoulder and neckband seam. Sew on sleeves, placing centre of sleeves to shoulder seams. Join side and sleeve seams.

# Moss and Cable Jacket with Petal Collar page 26

## MATERIALS

10(11: 14) 50g balls of Rowan DK Handknit Cotton.
Pair each of 3¼mm (No 10/US 3) and 4mm (No 8/US 6) knitting needles.
Cable needle.
7 buttons.

## MEASUREMENTS

| To fit age | 2-4 | 4-6 | 6-8 | years |
|---|---|---|---|---|
| Actual chest | 72 | 85 | 102 | cm |
| measurement | 28½ | 33½ | 40 | in |
| Length | 43 | 50 | 58 | cm |
| | 17 | 19¾ | 23 | in |
| Sleeve seam | 26 | 31 | 38 | cm |
| | 10¼ | 12¼ | 15 | in |

## TENSION

22 sts and 32 rows to 10cm/4in square over pattern on 4mm (No 8/US 6) needles.

## ABBREVIATIONS

See page 42.

## PANEL A

Worked over 4 sts.
**1st row (right side)** K4.
**2nd row** P4.
**3rd row** Sl next 2 sts onto cable needle and leave at front of work, k2, then k2 from cable needle.
**4th row** P4.
**5th and 6th rows** As 1st and 2nd rows.
These 6 rows form patt.

## PANEL B

Worked over 7 sts.
**1st row (right side)** K1, p1, k5.
**2nd row** P4, k1, p2.
**3rd row** [K1, p1] twice, k3.
**4th row** P2, k1, p1, k1, p2.
**5th row** [K1, p1] 3 times, k1.
**6th row** As 4th row.
**7th row** As 3rd row.
**8th row** As 2nd row.
**9th row** As 1st row.
**10th row** P7.
These 10 rows form patt.

## PANEL C

Worked over 7 sts.
**1st row (right side)** K5, p1, k1.
**2nd row** P2, k1, p4.
**3rd row** K3, [p1, k1] twice.
**4th row** P2, k1, p1, k1, p2.

**5th row** K1, [p1, k1] 3 times.
**6th row** As 4th row.
**7th row** As 3rd row.
**8th row** As 2nd row.
**9th row** As 1st row.
**10th row** P7.
These 10 rows form patt.

## BACK

With 3¼mm (No 10/US 3) needles cast on 75(89: 105) sts.
**1st row** K1(0: 0), [p1, k1] to last 0(1: 1) st, p0(1: 1).
This row forms moss st. Moss st 2 rows more.
**Next row** Moss st 5(12: 4), [m1, moss st 16] 4(4: 6) times, m1, moss st to end. 80(94: 112) sts.
Change to 4mm (No 8/US 6) needles.
**1st row (right side)** Moss st 1(1: 0), [work 1st row of panel B] 0(1: 0) time, [moss st 3, work 1st row of panel A, moss st 3, work 1st row of panel B] 2(2: 3) times, moss st 3, work 1st row of panel A, moss st 3, [work 1st row of panel C, moss st 3, work 1st row of panel A, moss st 3] 2(2: 3) times, [work 1st row of panel C] 0(1: 0) time, moss st 1(1: 0).
**2nd row** Moss st 1(1: 0), [work 2nd row of panel C] 0(1: 0) time, [moss st 3, work 2nd row of panel A, moss st 3, work 2nd row of

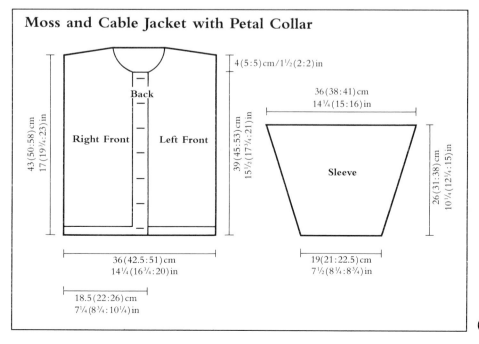

### Moss and Cable Jacket with Petal Collar

Back
Right Front — Left Front

43(50:58)cm
17(19¾:23)in

39(45:53)cm
15½(17¾:21)in

4(5:5)cm/1½(2:2)in

36(38:41)cm
14¼(15:16)in

Sleeve

26(31:38)cm
10¼(12¼:15)in

36(42.5:51)cm
14¼(16¾:20)in

18.5(22:26)cm
7¼(8¾:10¼)in

19(21:22.5)cm
7½(8¼:8¾)in

panel B, moss st 3, work 2nd row of panel A, moss st 3] 2(2: 3) times, [work 2nd row of panel B] 0(1: 0) time, moss st 1(1: 0).
These 2 rows set position of panels. Cont in patt until Back measures 43(50: 58)cm/17 (19¾: 23)in from beg, ending with a wrong side row.

### Shape Shoulders
Cast off 11(14: 18) sts at beg of next 2 rows and 12(15: 19) sts at beg of foll 2 rows. Leave rem 34(36: 38) sts on a holder.

### LEFT FRONT
With 3¼mm (No 10/US 3) needles cast on 39(46: 54) sts.
**1st row** K1(0: 0), [p1, k1] to end.
**2nd row** [K1, p1] to last 1(0: 0) st, k1(0: 0).
These 2 rows form moss st. Moss st 1 row.
**Next row** Moss st 17, [m1, moss st 16] 1(1: 2) times, m1, moss st to end. 41(48: 57) sts.
Change to 4mm (No 8/US 6) needles.
**1st row (right side)** Moss st 1(1: 0), [work 1st row of panel B] 0(1: 0) time, [moss st 3, work 1st row of panel A, moss st 3, work 1st row of panel B] 2(2: 3) times, moss st 6.
2nd row Moss st 6, [work 2nd row of panel B, moss st 3, work 2nd row of panel A, moss st 3] 2(2: 3) times, [work 2nd row of panel B] 0(1: 0) time, moss st 1(1: 0).
These 2 rows set position of panels. Cont in patt until Front measures 39(45: 53)cm/15½ (17¾: 21)in from beg, ending with a wrong side row.

### Shape Neck
**Next row** Patt to last 6 sts, turn; leave the 6 sts on a safety pin.
Keeping patt correct, work 1 row. Cast off 5 sts at beg of next row. Dec one st at neck edge on every row until 23(29: 37) sts rem.
Cont straight until Front matches Back to shoulder shaping, ending with a wrong side row.

### Shape Shoulder
Cast off 11(14: 18) sts at beg of next row.
Work 1 row. Cast off rem 12(15: 19) sts.
Mark front edge to indicate position of 7 buttons: first one 4 rows up from lower edge, last one 2 rows below neck shaping and rem 5 evenly spaced between.

### RIGHT FRONT
With 3¼mm (No 10/US 3) needles cast on 39(46: 54) sts.
**1st row** [K1, p1] to last 1(0: 0) st, k1(0: 0).
**2nd row** K1(0: 0), [p1, k1] to end.
These 2 rows form moss st. Moss st 1 row more.
**Next row** Moss st 5(12: 4), [m1, moss st 16] 2(2: 3) times, moss st 2. 41(48: 57) sts.
Change to 4mm (No 8/US 6) needles.
**1st (buttonhole) row (right side)** Moss st 2, k2 tog, yf, moss st 2, [work 1st row of panel C, moss st 3, work 1st row of panel A, moss st 3] 2(2: 3) times, [work 1st row of panel C] 0(1: 0) time, moss st 1(1: 0).
**2nd row** Moss st 1(1: 0), [work 2nd row of panel C] 0(1: 0) time, [moss st 3, work 2nd row of panel A, moss st 3, work 2nd row of panel C] 2(2: 3) times, moss st 6.
These 2 rows set position of panels.
Complete to match Left Front, making buttonholes to match markers and reversing shapings.

### SLEEVES
With 3¼mm (No 10/US 3) needles cast on 39(43: 47) sts.
Work 3 rows in moss st patt as given for 1st size on Back.
**Next row** Moss st 3(5: 7), [m1, moss st 16] twice, m1, moss st to end. 42(46: 50) sts.
Change to 4mm (No 8/US 6) needles.
**1st row (right side)** Moss st 2(4: 6), work 1st row of panel A, moss st 3, work 1st row of panel B, moss st 3, work 1st row of panel A, moss st 3, work 1st row of panel C, moss st 3, work 1st row of panel A, moss st 2(4: 6).
**2nd row** Moss st 2(4: 6), work 2nd row of panel A, moss st 3, work 2nd row of panel C, moss st 3, work 2nd row of panel A, moss st 3, work 2nd row of panel B, moss st 3, work 2nd row of panel A, moss st 2(4: 6).
These 2 rows set position of panels. Cont in patt, inc one st at each end of 3rd row and every foll 3rd(4th: 5th) row until there are 80(84: 90) sts, working incs into moss st.
Cont straight until Sleeve measures 26(31: 38)cm/10¼(12¼: 15)in from beg, ending with a wrong side row. Cast off.

### COLLAR
Join shoulder seams.
With 3¼mm (No 10/US 3) needles and right side facing, slip 6 sts from right front safety pin onto needle, k up 18(21: 21) sts up right front neck, work across back neck as follows: k0(1: 0), [k2 tog] 1(1: 2) times, moss st 5, work 3 tog, moss st 5, k1, k2 tog, k1, moss st 5, work 3 tog, moss st 5, [k2 tog] 1(1: 2) times, k0(1: 0), k up 18(21: 21) sts down left front neck, moss st 6 sts from left front safety pin. 75(83: 83) sts. Cont in moss st, work 1 row. Cast off 3 sts at beg of next 2 rows. 69(77: 77) sts.
**Next row** Moss st 4(3: 3), work into front, back and front of next st, [moss st 5(6: 6), work into front, back and front of next st] 10 times, moss st to end. 91(99:99)sts. Moss st 6 rows.
**★★Next row** Moss st 9 and turn.
Work on these 9 sts only. Dec one st at each end of next row and 2 foll alt rows. Patt 1 row. Work 3 tog and fasten off. Rejoin yarn to rem sts and rep ★★ until all sts are worked off and dec one st at beg of making 6th point on **1st size only**.

### TO MAKE UP
Sew on sleeves, placing centre of sleeves to shoulder seams. Join side and sleeve seams, Sew on buttons.

# Fair Isle Sweater

## MATERIALS
5(6: 7) balls of Rowan DK Hanknit Cotton in Maroon (A).
3(4: 5) balls of same in Black (B).
2(2: 3) balls of same in Green.
1 ball of same in each of Pink, Blue, Lime, Lilac and White.
Pair each of 3¼mm (No 10/US 3) and 4mm (No 8/US 6) knitting needles.

## MEASUREMENTS

| To fit age | 5–7 | 7–9 | 9–11 years | |
|---|---|---|---|---|
| Actual chest measurement | 90 | 100 | 112 | cm |
| | 35½ | 39½ | 44 | in |
| Length | 45 | 53 | 57 | cm |
| | 17¾ | 21 | 22½ | in |
| Sleeve seam | 31 | 36 | 41 | cm |
| | 12¼ | 14¼ | 16 | in |

## TENSION
22 sts and 25 rows to 10cm/4in square over pattern on 4mm (No 8/US 6) needles.

## ABBREVIATIONS
<blockquote>See page 42.</blockquote>

## NOTES
Read chart from right to left on right side (k) rows and from left to right on wrong side (p) rows. When working in rib or pattern, strand yarn not in use loosely across wrong side over no more than 5 sts at the time to keep fabric elastic.

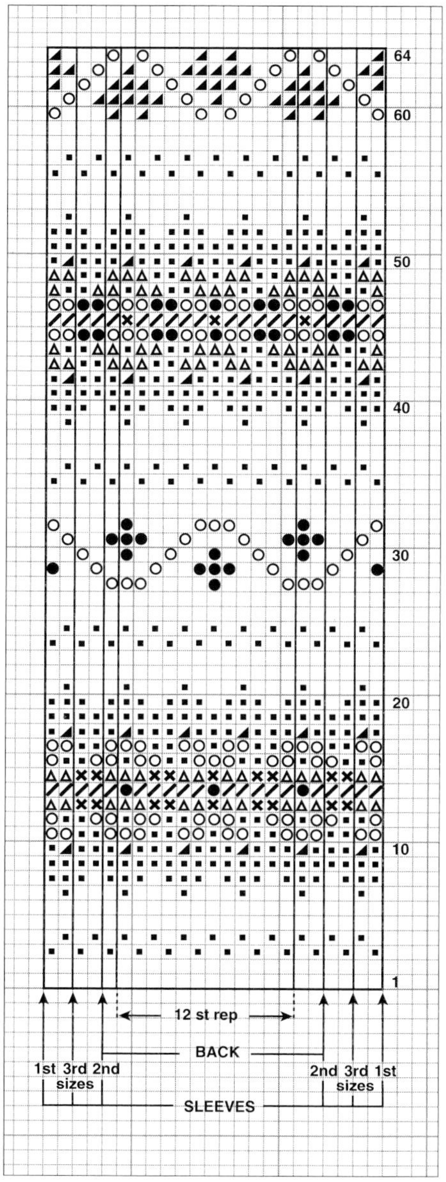

## BACK

With 3¼mm (No 10/US 3) needles and A, cast on 98(110: 122) sts.
Beg with a k row, work 4 rows in st st.
**1st rib row (right side)** P2A, [k2B, p2A] to end.
**2nd rib row** K2A, [p2B, k2A] to end.
Rep last 2 rows twice more, inc one st at centre of last row. 99(111: 123) sts.
Change to 4mm (No 8/US 6) needles.
Beg with a k row, work in st st and patt from chart until Back measures 45(53: 57)cm/17¾(21: 22½)in from beg, ending with a wrong side row.
**Shape Shoulders**
Cast off 16(18: 20) sts at beg of next 4 rows.
Leave rem 35(39: 43) sts on a holder.

## FRONT

Work as given for Back until Front measures 38(46: 50)cm/15(18¼: 19¾)in from beg, ending with a wrong side row.
**Shape Neck**
**Next row** Patt 40(44: 48), turn.
Work on this set of sts only. Keeping patt correct, dec one st at neck edge on next 4 rows, then on 4 foll alt rows. 32(36: 40) sts.
Cont straight until Front matches Back to shoulder shaping, ending at side edge.

## KEY

| | |
|---|---|
| ☐ | Maroon (A) |
| ■ | Black |
| O | Green |
| ◢ | Pink |
| △ | Blue |
| ✖ | Lime |
| ● | Lilac |
| ◪ | White |

## Shape Shoulder

Cast off 16(18: 20) sts at beg of next row.
Work 1 row. Cast off rem 16(18: 20) sts.
With right side facing, slip centere 19(23: 27) sts onto holder, rejoin yarn to rem sts, patt to end. Complete to match first side of neck.

## SLEEVES

With 3¼mm (No 10/US 3) needles and A, cast on 46(50: 54) sts.
Beg with a k row, work 4 rows in st st, then 4 rows in rib as given for Back, inc one st at centre of last row. 47(51: 55) sts.
Change to 4mm (No 8/US 6) needles.
Beg with a k row, work in st st and patt from chart, at the same time, inc one st at each end of 3rd row and every foll 4th(5th: 6th) row until there are 73(79: 85) sts, working inc sts into patt. Cont straight until Sleeve measures 31(36: 41)cm/12¼(14¼: 16)in from beg, ending with a wrong side row. Cast off.

## NECKBAND

Join right shoulder seam.
With 3¼mm (No 10/US 3) needles, A and right side facing, k up 16 sts down left front neck, k centre front neck sts, k up 16 sts up right front neck, k back neck sts. 86(94: 102) sts. Beg with a 2nd row, work 4 rows in rib as given for Back. Cont in A only. Beg with a p row, work 4 rows in st st.
Cast off loosely.

## TO MAKE UP

Join left shoulder and neckband seam, reversing seam on st st section of neckband. Sew on sleeves, placing centre of sleeves to shoulder seams. Join side and sleeve seams, reversing seams on first and last 4 rows.

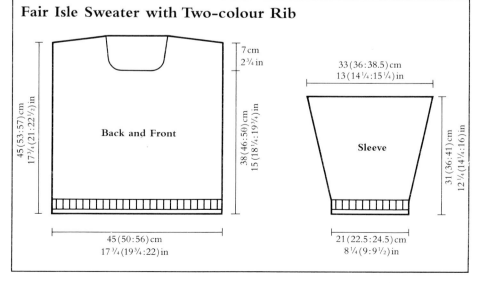

**Fair Isle Sweater with Two-colour Rib**

Back and Front
45(53:57)cm 17¾(21:22½)in
7 cm 2¾ in
38(46:50)cm 15(18¼:19¾)in
45(50:56)cm 17¾(19¾:22)in

Sleeve
33(36:38.5)cm 13(14¼:15¼)in
31(36:41)cm 12¼(14¼:16)in
21(22.5:24.5)cm 8¼(9:9½)in

## MATERIALS

11(12: 14) 50g balls of Rowan Cotton Glace.
Pair each of 3mm (No 11/US 2) and 3¼mm (No 10/US 3) knitting needles.
One 3 1/4mm (No 10/US 3) circular needle.
Cable needle.

## MEASUREMENTS

| To fit age | 3-4 | 6-8 | 8-10 years | |
|---|---|---|---|---|
| Actual chest | 80 | 95 | 110 | cm |
| measurement | 31½ | 37½ | 43½ | in |
| Length | 45 | 52 | 61 | cm |
| | 17¾ | 20½ | 24 | in |
| Sleeve seam | 29 | 34 | 40 | cm |
| | 11½ | 13½ | 15¾ | in |

## TENSION

28 sts and 40 rows to 10cm/4in square over pattern on 3¼mm (No 10/US 3) needles.

## ABBREVIATIONS

**C4B** = sl next 2 sts onto cable needle and leave at back of work, k2, then k2 from cable needle;
**Cr3L** = sl next 2 sts onto cable needle and leave at front of work, p1, then k2 from cable needle;
**Cr3R** = sl next st onto cable needle and leave at back of work, k2, then p1 from cable needle;
**mb** = p into front, back, front, back, front, then k into back of next st, pass 2nd, 3rd, 4th, 5th and 6th st over 1st st.
Also see page 42.

## PANEL A

Worked over 7 sts.
**1st row (right side)** P7.
**2nd row** P7.
**3rd row** P3, mb, p3.
**4th, 5th and 6th rows** P7.
These 6 rows form patt.

## PANEL B

Worked over 14 sts.
**1st row (right side)** P5, C4B, p5.
**2nd row** K5, p4, k5.
**3rd row** P4, Cr3R, Cr3L, p4.
**4th row** K4, p6, k4.
**5th row** P3, Cr3R, p2, Cr3L, p3.
**6th row** K3, p8, k3.
**7th row** P2, Cr3R, p4, Cr3L, p2.
**8th row** K2, p10, k2.
**9th row** P1, Cr3R, p6, Cr3L, p1.
**10th row** K1, p12, k1.
**11th row** P1, Cr3L, p6, Cr3R, p1.
**12th row** As 8th row.
**13th row** P2, Cr3L, p4, Cr3R, p2.
**14th row** As 6th row.
**15th row** P3, Cr3L, p2, Cr3R, p3.
**16th row** As 4th row.
**17th row** P4, Cr3L, Cr3R, p4.
**18th row** As 2nd row.
**19th and 20th rows** As 1st and 2nd rows.
**21st row** P5, k4, p5.
**22nd row** As 2nd row.
These 22 rows form patt.

## BACK

Begin at shoulders.
With 3¼mm (No 10/US 3) needles cast on 112(133: 154) sts.
**1st row (right side)** Work 1st row of panel A, [work 1st row of panel B, then panel A] to end.
This row sets position of panels. Cont in patt until Back measures approximately 43(50: 59)cm/17(19¾: 23¼)in from beg, ending with 19th(1st: 19th) row of panel B.
P 1 row, dec 2 sts over each cable. 102(121: 140) sts.
Change to 3mm (No 11/US 2) needles.
P 5 rows.

**Next row** P2(3: 3), [p2 tog, p4] to last 4(4: 5) sts, p2 tog, p2(2: 3). 85(101: 117) sts.
**Next row** Cast off purlwise 2 sts, [sl st used in casting off back onto left hand needle, cast on 2 sts purlwise, cast off 4 sts purlwise] to end.
Fasten off.

## FRONT

Begin at left shoulder.
With 3¼mm (No 10/US 3) needles cast on 38(46: 54) sts.
**1st size only**
**1st row (right side)** P1, C4B, p5, work 1st row of panel A, then panel B and panel A.
**2nd row** Work 2nd row of panel A, then panel B and panel A, k5, p4, k1.
**2nd size only**
**1st row (right side)** P4, [work 1st row of panel B, then panel A] twice.
**2nd row** [Work 2nd row of panel A, then panel B] twice, p4.
**3rd size only**
**1st row (right side)** P5, work 1st row of panel A, [work 1st row of panel B, then panel A] twice.
**2nd row** [Work 2nd row of panel A, then panel B] twice, work 2nd row of panel A, k5.
**All sizes**
These 2 rows set position of panels. Cont in patt, inc one st at beg of 5th row and at same edge on every foll 7th row until there are 46(56: 66) sts, working inc sts into patt. Patt 8(6: 4) rows straight. Leave these sts on a spare needle.
With 3¼mm (No 10/US 3) needle cast on 38(46: 54) sts for right side of neck.
**1st size only**
**1st row (right side)** Work 1st row of panel A, then panel B and panel A, p5, C4B, p1.
**2nd row** K1, p4, k5, work 2nd row of panel A, then panel B and panel A.
**2nd size only**
**1st row (right side)** [Work 1st row of panel A, then panel B] twice, p4.
**2nd row** P4, [work 2nd row of panel B, then panel A] twice.

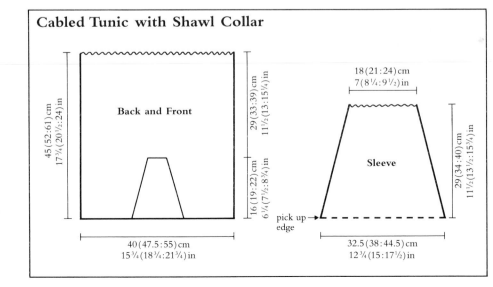

## Cabled Tunic with Shawl Collar

Back and Front

45(52:61)cm
17¾(20½:24)in

29(33:39)cm
11½(13:15¼)in

16(19:22)cm
6¼(7½:8¾)in

40(47.5:55)cm
15¾(18¾:21¾)in

18(21:24)cm
7(8¼:9½)in

Sleeve

29(34:40)cm
11½(13½:15¾)in

pick up edge

32.5(38:44.5)cm
12¾(15:17½)in

**3rd size only**
**1st row (right side)** Work 1st row of panel A, [work 1st row of panel B, then panel A] twice, p5.
**2nd row** K5, work 2nd row of panel A, [work 2nd row of panel B, then panel A] twice.
**All sizes**
These 2 rows set position of panels. Cont in patt, inc one st at end of 5th row and at same edge on every foll 7th row until there are 46(56: 66) sts, working inc sts into patt. Patt 8(6: 4) rows straight.
**Next row** Patt to end, cast on 20(21: 22) sts, then patt across sts on spare needle. 112(133: 154) sts.
Mark each end of last row. Complete as given for Back.

**SLEEVES**
Join shoulder seams. Mark same row at side edges of Back as on Front.
With 3¼mm (No 10/US 3) needles and right side facing, k up 91(106: 125) sts between markers.

**1st row (wrong side)** P7(4: 3), work 22nd row of panel B, [work 6th row of panel A, work 22nd row of panel B] to last 7(4: 3) sts, p7(4: 3).
**2nd row** P7(4: 3), work 1st row of panel B, [work 1st row of panel A, then panel B] to last 7(4: 3) sts, p7(4: 3).
These 2 rows set position of panels. Cont in patt, dec one st at each end of 9th(9th: 7th) row, then every foll 5th row until 51(58: 67) sts rem. Patt 2(4: 3) rows straight.
**1st size only**
**Next row** P7, *p2 tog, p4, [p2 tog] twice, p4, p2 tog, p5; rep from * once more, p2.
**2nd and 3rd sizes only**
**Next row** [P2 tog, p4] 1(0) time, ** [p2 tog] twice, p4, p2 tog, p5, p2 tog, p4; rep from * 1(2) times more, [p2 tog] twice, p6(0).
**All sizes**
43(47: 53) sts.
Change to 3mm (No 11/US 2) needles.
P 5 rows.
**Next row** P3(5: 3), [p2 tog, p3] to last 5(7: 5) sts, p2 tog, p3(5: 3). 35(39: 43) sts.
Cast off as given for Back.

**COLLAR**
With 3 1/4mm (No 10/US 3) circular needle and right side facing, k up 47(56: 65) sts up right front neck, 32(36: 42) sts across back neck and 47(56: 65) sts down left front neck. 126(148: 172) sts. Work backwards and forwards in rows. K 27(29: 31) rows, dec 5(7: 9) sts evenly across last row. 121(141: 163) sts.
**Next row** Cast off knitwise 2 sts, [sl st used in casting off back onto left hand needle, cast on 2 sts knitwise, cast off 4 sts knitwise] to end.
Fasten off.

**TO MAKE UP**
Beginning 6cm/2¼in up from lower edge, join side seams, then sleeve seams. Lap right side of collar over left side and catch down row ends of collar together to cast on sts at centre of front.

# Shawl-collared Jacket with Fair Isle Bands page 29

## MATERIALS
3(4: 6: 7: 8) 50g balls of Rowan Cotton Glace in Cream (A).
1(1: 2: 2: 2) balls of same in Beige.
1(1: 1: 2: 2) balls of same in Pink.
1(1: 1: 1: 2) balls of same in Light Blue.
1 ball of same in Dark Blue.
Pair each of 3mm (No 11/US 2) and 3¼mm (No 10/US 3) knitting needles.
8(8: 9: 9: 10) buttons.

## TENSION
26 sts and 33 rows to 10cm/4in square over pattern on 3¼mm (No 10/US 3) needles.

## ABBREVIATIONS
See page 42

## NOTES
Read chart from right to left on right side (k) rows and from left to right on wrong side (p) rows. When working in pattern, strand yarn not in use loosely across wrong side of work to keep fabric elastic.

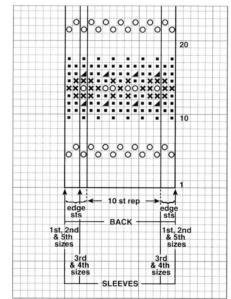

## KEY
| | |
|---|---|
| ☐ | Cream (A) |
| ▪ | Beige |
| ◯ | Pink |
| ✕ | Light Blue |
| ◤ | Dark Blue |

## BACK AND FRONTS
Worked in one piece to armholes.
With 3mm (No 11/US 2) needles and A, cast on 155(175: 195: 215: 235) sts.
**Next row** K1, [p1, k1] to end.
This row forms moss st. Moss st 1 row.
**Buttonhole row** Moss st 2, yrn, p2 tog, patt to end.
Moss st 1 row.
**Next row** Moss st 5 and sl these 5 sts onto safety pin, moss st to last 5 sts, sl last 5 sts onto safety pin. 145(165: 185: 205: 225) sts. Change to 3¼mm (No 10/US 3) needles. Beg with a p row, cont in st st and patt from chart until work measures 17(19: 21: 23: 27)cm/6 3/4(7½: 8¼: 9: 10½)in from beg, ending with a wrong side row.

## MEASUREMENTS
| To fit age | 1 | 2 | 3-4 | 4-6 | 6-8 | years |
|---|---|---|---|---|---|---|
| Actual chest | 58 | 65 | 73 | 80 | 88 | cm |
| measurement | 22¾ | 25½ | 28¾ | 31½ | 34½ | in |
| Length | 29 | 33 | 36 | 40 | 45 | cm |
| | 11½ | 13 | 14¼ | 15¾ | 17¾ | in |
| Sleeve seam | 19 | 23 | 28 | 32 | 38 | cm |
| | 7½ | 9 | 11 | 12½ | 15 | in |

## Right Front

**Next row** Patt 35(40: 45: 50: 55), turn. Work on this set of sts only.

**Shape Neck**
Keeping patt correct, dec one st at neck edge on every 3rd row until 24(28: 32: 36: 40) sts rem. Cont straight until Front measures 29(33: 36: 40: 45)cm/11 1/2(13: 14 ¼: 15¾: 17¾)in from beg, ending at armhole edge.

**Shape Shoulder**
Cast off 12(14: 16: 18: 20) sts at beg of next row. Work 1 row. Cast off rem 12(14: 16: 18: 20) sts.

**Back**
With right side facing, rejoin yarn to rem sts, patt 75(85: 95: 105: 115) sts, turn. Work straight on this set of sts only until Back matches Front to shoulder shaping, ending with a wrong side row.

**Shape Shoulders**
Cast off 12(14: 16: 18: 20) sts at beg of next 4 rows. Leave rem 27(29: 31: 33: 35) sts on a holder.

**Left Front**
With right side facing, rejoin yarn to rem sts and patt to end. Complete as given for Right Front.

## SLEEVES

With 3mm (No 11/US 2) needles and A, cast on 35(37: 39: 41: 43) sts.
Work 4 rows in moss st.
**Next row** Moss st 4(4: 3: 2: 5), m1, [moss st 3(4: 3: 4: 3), m1] to last 4(5: 3: 3: 5), moss st to end. 45(45: 51: 51: 55) sts.
Change to 3¼mm (No 10/US 3) needles. Beg with a p row, work in st st and patt from chart, at the same time, inc one st at each end of 3rd row and every foll 4th(4th: 5th: 4th: 5th) row until there are 65(73: 81: 89: 97) sts, working inc sts into patt. Cont straight until Sleeve measures 19(23: 28: 32: 38)cm/7½(9: 11: 12½: 15)in from beg, ending wirh a wrong side row. Cast off

## BUTTON BAND AND LEFT COLLAR

With 3mm (No 11/US 2) needles, rejoin A yarn at inside edge to 5 sts on left front safety pin, inc in first st, moss st to end. Cont in moss st until band, when slightly stretched, fits up left front to beg of neck shaping.

**Shape Collar**
Inc and work into moss st, one st at inside edge on next row and every foll 4th row until there are 15 sts. Cont straight until collar fits left front neck to shoulder, ending at outside edge.
**Next 2 rows** Moss st 9, turn, sl 1, moss st to end.
Moss st 6 rows. Rep last 8 rows until collar fits left front neck to centre of back neck. Cast off.
Mark band to indicate position of 4(4: 5: 5: 6) buttons: first one to match buttonhole already made on right front welt, last one 2 rows below collar shaping and rem 2(2: 3: 3: 4) evenly spaced between.

## BUTTONHOLE BAND AND RIGHT COLLAR

Work as given for Button Band and Left Collar, making buttonholes to match markers as before.

## SIDE BELTS (make 2)

With 3mm (No 11/US 2) needles and A, cast on 7 sts.
Work in moss st for 8(8: 9: 9: 10)cm/3(3: 3½: 3½: 4)in. Cast off.

## TO MAKE UP

Join shoulder seams. Sew in sleeves. Join sleeve seams. Sew on front bands and collar in place, then join back seam of collar. Sew on buttons. Place side belts where desired at each side and secure in positions with buttons.

# Navy and Cream Striped Top page 30

## MATERIALS
3(4: 5: 6: 7: 8) 50g balls of Rowan Cotton Glace in each of Navy (A) and Cream (B).
Pair of 2¾mm (No 12/US 2) knitting needles.
Pair of 3¼mm (No 10/US 3) double pointed knitting needles.
3(3: 4: 4: 5: 5) buttons.

## TENSION
25 sts and 36 rows to 10cm/4in square over st st on 3¼mm (No 10/US 3) needles.

## ABBREVIATIONS
See page 42.

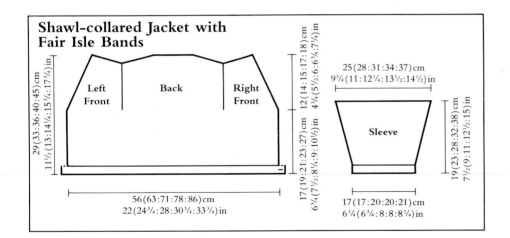

**Shawl-collared Jacket with Fair Isle Bands**

Left Front — Back — Right Front

29(33: 36: 40: 45)cm
11½ (13: 14¼: 15¾: 17¾)in

12(14: 15: 17: 18)cm
4¾(5½: 6: 6¾: 7¼)in

17(19: 21: 23: 27)cm
6¾(7½: 8¼: 9: 10½)in

56(63: 71: 78: 86)cm
22(24¾: 28: 30¾: 33¾)in

25(28: 31: 34: 37)cm
9¾(11: 12¼: 13½: 14½)in

Sleeve

19(23: 28: 32: 38)cm
7½(9: 11: 12½: 15)in

17(17: 20: 20: 21)cm
6¾(6¾: 8: 8: 8¼)in

## BACK

With 2¾mm (No 12/US 2) needles and A, cast on 81(89: 105: 115: 127: 139) sts. K 7 rows.
Change to 3¼mm (No 10/US 3) needles.
**Next row (right side)** K4, turn.
Work on these 4 sts only. K 5(5: 9: 9: 13: 13) rows. Leave these sts on a safety pin.
With right side facing, join B to rem sts, k to last 4 sts, turn.
Work on this set of sts only in stripe patt as follows:
**1st row** Return to beg of last row, with A, k to end.
**2nd row** With B, p to end.
**3rd row** Return to beg of last row, with A, p to end.
**4th row** With B, k to end.
The last 4 rows form stripe patt. Patt a further 1(1: 5: 5: 9: 9) rows. Leave these sts on a spare needle.
With right side facing, rejoin A to rem 4 sts and k 6(6: 10: 10: 14: 14) rows. Slip these sts onto needle holding centre sts.
With wrong side facing and B, p across all sts.
Beg with a 3rd row, cont in stripe patt until Back measures approximately 22(26: 30: 36: 39: 43)cm/8¾(10 1/4: 11¾: 14¼: 15¼: 17)in from beg, ending with 3rd row of stripe patt.★★
**Next row** With B, k6, p5, k to last 11 sts, p5, k6.
**Next row** Return to beg of last row, with A, k6, p5, k to last 11 sts, p5, k6.
**Next row** With B, p6, k5, p to last 11 sts, k5, p6.
**Next row** Return to beg of last row, with A, p6, k5, p to last 11 sts, k5, p6.
Rep last 4 rows for a further 6(7: 9: 10: 11: 13)cm/2¼(2¾: 3½: 4: 4¼: 5)in, ending with 4th row of the last 4 rows.
Beg with 4th row, work in stripe patt until Back measures approximately 31(36: 43: 50: 55: 61)cm/12¼(14: 17: 19¾: 21½: 24)in from beg, ending with 3rd row of stripe patt.
### Shape Neck
**Next row** Patt 29(32: 39: 43: 48: 53), turn.
Work on this set of sts only. Dec one st at neck edge on next 4 rows. 25(28: 35: 39: 44: 49) sts. Patt 1 row. Cast off.
With right side facing, slip centre 23(25: 27: 29: 31: 33) sts onto a holder, rejoin yarn to rem sts, patt to end. Complete as given for first side.

## FRONT

Work as given for Back to ★★
### Divide for Opening
**Next row** With B, k6, p5, k27(31: 39: 43: 49: 55), turn.
Work on this set of sts only.
**Next row** Return to beg of last row, with A, k6, p5, k to end.
**Next row** With B, p to last 11 sts, k5, p6.
**Next row** Return to beg of last row, with A, p to last 11 sts, k5, p6.
**Next row** With B, k6, p5, k to end.
Rep last 4 rows for a further 6(7: 9: 10: 11: 13)cm/2¼(2 3/4: 3½: 4: 4¼: 5)in, ending with 3rd row of the last 4 rows.
Beg with 4th row, cont in stripe patt, work 2 rows.
### Shape Neck
Cast off 7(8: 8: 8: 9: 9) sts at beg of next row. Dec one st at neck edge on every row until 25(28: 35: 39: 44: 49) sts rem. Cont straight until Front matches Back to cast off edge. Cast off.

With right side facing, rejoin B to rem sts, cast off centre 5(5: 5: 7: 7: 7) sts, k to last 11 sts, p5, k6.
**Next row** Return to beg of last row, with A, k to last 11 sts, p5, k6.
**Next row** With B, p6, k5, p to end.
**Next row** Return to beg of last row, with A, p6, k5, p to end.
**Next row** With B, k to last 11 sts, p5, k6.
Complete to match first side, reversing shaping.

## SLEEVES

With 2 3/4mm (No 12/US 2) needles and A, cast on 40(42: 44: 48: 50: 52) sts.
K 7 rows, inc 4 sts evenly across last row. 44(46: 48: 52: 54: 56) sts.
Change to 3¼mm (No 10/US 3) needles.
Work in stripe patt as given for Back, inc one st at each end of 3rd row and every foll 5th(4th: 4th: 4th: 4th: 4th) row until there are 66(76: 86: 96: 106: 116) sts. Cont straight until Sleeve measures 20(23: 28: 32: 38: 40)cm/8(9: 11: 12½: 15: 15¾)in from beg. Cast off.

## BUTTONHOLE BAND

With 2 3/4mm (No 12/US 2) needles, A and right side facing, k up 18(21: 26: 30: 33: 38) sts evenly along right edge of front opening. K 2(2: 2: 3: 3: 3) rows.
**Buttonhole row** K5(6: 5: 5: 3: 4), [yf, k2 tog, k6(7: 6: 7: 6: 7)] 1(1: 2: 2: 3: 3) times, yf, k2 tog, k to end.
K 3(3: 3: 4: 4: 4) rows. Cast off.

## BUTTON BAND

Work to match Buttonhole Band, omitting buttonholes.

## NECKBAND

Join shoulder seams.
With 2¾mm (No 12/US 2) needles, A and right side facing, k up 19(20: 22: 22: 25: 25) sts up right front neck, 6 sts down right back neck, k centre back neck sts dec 2 sts, k up 6 sts up left back neck and 19(20: 22: 22: 25: 25) sts down left front neck. 71(75: 81: 83: 91: 93) sts. K 2 rows.
**Buttonhole row** K to last 4 sts, k2 tog, yf, k2.
K 3 rows. Cast off.

## TO MAKE UP

Sew side edge edgings to main part. Sew on sleeves, placing centre of sleeves to shoulder seams. Beginning at top of side edgings, join side seams, then sleeve seams. Lap buttonhole band over button band and catch together row end edges to base of opening. Sew on buttons.

## MEASUREMENTS

| To fit age | 1 | 1–2 | 3–4 | 4–6 | 6–8 | 8–10 | years |
|---|---|---|---|---|---|---|---|
| Actual chest | 64 | 71 | 84 | 92 | 102 | 111 | cm |
| measurement | 25 | 28 | 33 | 36 | 40 | 43½ | in |
| Length | 32 | 37 | 44 | 51 | 56 | 62 | cm |
| | 12¾ | 14½ | 17½ | 20¼ | 22 | 24½ | in |
| Sleeve seam | 20 | 23 | 28 | 32 | 38 | 40 | cm |
| | 8 | 9 | 11 | 12½ | 15 | 15¾ | in |

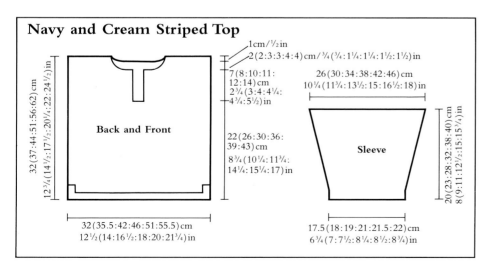

**Navy and Cream Striped Top**

Back and Front

32(37: 44: 51: 56: 62) cm
12¾(14½: 17½: 20¼: 22: 24½) in

1cm/½in
2(2:3:3:4:4) cm/¾(¾:1¼:1¼:1½:1½) in
7(8:10:11: 12:14) cm
2¾(3:4:4¼: 4¾:5½) in
22(26:30:36: 39:43) cm
8¾(10¼:11¾: 14¼:15¼:17) in
32(35.5:42:46:51:55.5) cm
12½(14:16½:18:20:21¾) in

Sleeve

26(30:34:38:42:46) cm
10¼(11¾:13½:15:16½:18) in
20(23:28:32:38:40) cm
8(9:11:12½:15:15¾) in
17.5(18:19:21:21.5:22) cm
6¾(7:7½:8¼:8½:8¾) in

71

## MATERIALS

4(4: 5: 5: 6) 100g hanks of Rowan Magpie Aran.
Small amount of DK yarn in Brown for embroidery.
Pair of 4½mm (No 7/US 7) knitting needles.
6 buttons.

## TENSION

18 sts and 38 rows to 10cm/4in square over garter st (every row k) on 4½mm (No 7/US 7) needles.

## ABBREVIATIONS

See page 42.

## BACK

With 4½ mm (No 7/US 7) needles cast on 70(74: 78: 82: 86) sts.
Work in garter st until Back measures 33(35: 37: 39: 41)cm/13(13¾: 14 1/2: 15¼: 16¼)in from beg.
**Shape Neck**
★★ Next 2 rows K26(27: 28: 30: 31), sl 1, yf, turn, sl 1, k to end.
Next 2 rows K23(24: 25: 27: 28), sl 1, yf, turn, sl 1, k to end.
Next 2 rows K20(21: 22: 24: 25), sl 1, yf, turn, sl 1, k to end.
K 1 row across all sts.★★ Rep from ★★ to ★★. Cast off.

## POCKET LININGS (make 2)

With 4½mm (No 7/US 7) needles cast on 23(24: 25: 27: 28) sts.
K 22(24: 26: 28: 30) rows. Leave these sts on a spare needle.

## LEFT FRONT

With 4½mm (No 7/US 7) needles cast on 38(40: 42: 44: 46) sts.
K 37(39: 41: 43: 45) rows.
**Place Pocket**
Next row (wrong side) K9(9: 10: 10: 10), cast off next 23(24: 25: 27: 28) sts, k to end.
Next row K6(7: 7: 7: 8), k across sts of pocket lining, k to end.
Cont in garter st across all sts until Front measures 31(33: 35: 37: 39)cm/12 1/4(13: 13¾: 14½: 15½)in from beg, ending with a wrong side row.
**Shape Neck**
1st row K29(30: 31: 33: 34), sl 1, yf, turn.
2nd row and 5 foll alt rows Sl 1, k to end.
3rd row K27(28: 29: 31: 32), sl 1, yf, turn.
5th row K25(26: 27: 29: 30), sl 1, yf, turn.
7th row K23(24: 25: 27: 28), sl 1, yf, turn.
9th row K22(23: 24: 26: 27), sl 1, yf, turn.
11th row K21(22: 23: 25: 26), sl 1, yf, turn.
13th row K20(21: 22: 24: 25), sl 1, yf, turn.
14th row As 2nd row.
K 2 rows across all sts. Cast off.
Mark front edge to indicate position of 6 buttons: first one 4 rows up from lower edge, last one 2 rows below neck shaping and rem 4 evenly spaced between.

## RIGHT FRONT

With 4½mm (No 7/US 7) needles cast on 38(40: 42: 44: 46) sts.
K 4 rows.
**Buttonhole row (right side)** K3, yf, k2 tog, k to end.
Complete as given for Left Front, making buttonholes to match markers, ending with a right side row before shaping neck and placing pocket as follows:
Next row (wrong side) K6(7: 7: 7: 8), cast off next 23(24: 25: 27: 28) sts, k to end.
Next row K9(9: 10: 10: 10), k across sts of pocket lining, k to end.

## SLEEVES

With 4½mm (No 7/US 7) needles cast on 41(43: 45: 47: 49) sts. Work in garter st for 12cm/4¾in. Cont in garter st, inc one st at each end of next row and every foll 6th(7th: 7th: 9th: 9th) row until there are 57(59: 63: 67: 75) sts. Cont straight until Sleeve measures 28(30: 33: 38: 46)cm/11(12: 13: 15: 18)in from beg. Cast off.

## TO MAKE UP

Join shoulder seams. Sew on sleeves, placing centre of sleeves to shoulder seams. Join side and sleeve seams, reversing seam on cuffs. Turn back cuffs. Catch down pocket linings. Sew on buttons. With Brown, embroider cross stitch on cuffs and pockets.

## MEASUREMENTS

| To fit age | 2-3 | 3-4 | 4-6 | 6-8 | 8-10 | years |
|---|---|---|---|---|---|---|
| Actual chest | 78 | 82 | 86 | 91 | 96 | cm |
| measurement | 31 | 32 | 34 | 36 | 38 | in |
| Length | 35 | 37 | 39 | 41 | 43 | cm |
| | 13¾ | 14½ | 15¼ | 16 | 17 | in |
| Sleeve seam (with cuff turned back) | 22 | 24 | 27 | 32 | 40 | cm |
| | 8¾ | 9¾ | 10¾ | 12¾ | 15¾ | in |

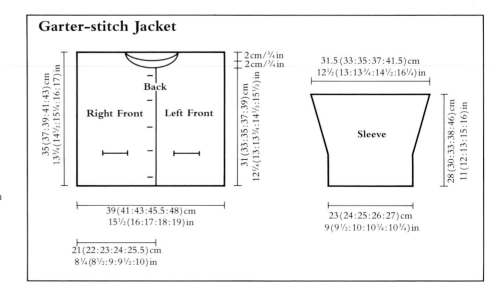

**Garter-stitch Jacket**

35(37:39:41:43)cm
13¾(14½:15¼:16:17)in

Back

Right Front | Left Front

2cm/¾in
2cm/¾in

31(33:35:37:39)cm
12¼(13:13¾:14½:15½)in

39(41:43:45.5:48)cm
15½(16:17:18:19)in

21(22:23:24:25.5)cm
8¼(8½:9:9½:10)in

31.5(33:35:37:41.5)cm
12½(13:13¾:14½:16¼)in

Sleeve

28(30:33:38:46)cm
11(12:13:15:16)in

23(24:25:26:27)cm
9(9½:10:10¼:10¾)in

# Simple Sweater with Shoulder Seam Detail page 32

## MATERIALS
4(4: 5: 5: 6: 6) 100g hanks of Rowan Magpie Aran.
Pair of 4½mm (No 7/US 7) knitting needles.

## TENSION
18 sts and 26 rows to 10cm/4in square over st st on 4½mm (No 7/US 7) needles.

## ABBREVIATIONS
See page 42

## BACK
With 4½mm (No 7/US 7) needles cast on 70(76: 82: 86: 94: 102) sts.
Work in st st until Back measures 43(46: 49: 53: 57: 60)cm/17(18: 19¼: 21: 22½: 23½)in from beg, ending with a p row. Leave these sts on a spare needle.

## FRONT
Work as given for Back until Front is 12(12: 12: 14: 14: 14) rows less than Back, ending with a p row.
**Shape Neck**
**Next row** K30(33: 35: 36: 39: 42), turn.
Work on this set of sts only. Cast off 3 sts at beg of next row. Dec one st at neck edge on every row until 22(24: 26: 27: 30: 33) sts rem. Work 5(4: 4: 6: 6: 6) rows straight. Leave these sts on a spare needle.
With right side facing, slip centre 10(10: 12: 14: 16: 18) sts onto a holder, rejoin yarn to rem sts and k to end. P 1 row. Complete to match first side.

## SLEEVES
With 4½mm (No 7/US 7) needles cast on 32(32: 34: 36: 36: 38) sts.
Work in st st, inc one st at each end of 7th row and every foll 4th row until there are 62(64: 68: 74: 78: 82) sts. Cont straight until Sleeve measures 28(30: 32: 37: 40: 42)cm/11(11¾: 12½: 14½: 15¾: 16½)in from beg. Cast off.

## NECKBAND
Place 22(24: 26: 27: 30: 33) sts of right back shoulder onto separate needle. With wrong sides of back and front together and right side of front facing, k tog right shoulder sts, then cast off.
With 4½mm (No 7/US 7) needles and right side facing, k up 13(13: 13: 15: 15: 15) sts down left front neck, k centre front sts, k up 13(13: 13: 15: 15: 15) sts up right front neck, then k26(28: 30: 32: 34: 36) sts of centre back neck, turn. 62(64: 68: 76: 80: 84) sts. Beg with a p row, work 9(9: 9: 11: 11: 11) rows in st st. Cast off loosely.

## TO MAKE UP
Join together left shoulder in same way as right shoulder, then join neckband seam, reversing seam on last 5 rows. Sew on sleeves, placing centre of sleeves to shoulder seams. Join side and sleeve seams, reversing seams on first and last 4 rows.

## MEASUREMENTS

| To fit age | 2-3 | 3-4 | 4-6 | 6-8 | 8-9 | 9-10 | years |
|---|---|---|---|---|---|---|---|
| Actual chest | 78 | 84 | 91 | 95 | 104 | 113 | cm |
| measurement | 30½ | 33 | 36 | 37½ | 41 | 44½ | in |
| Length | 43 | 46 | 49 | 53 | 57 | 60 | cm |
| | 17 | 18 | 19¼ | 21 | 22½ | 23½ | in |
| Sleeve seam | 28 | 30 | 32 | 37 | 40 | 42 | cm |
| | 11 | 11¾ | 12½ | 14½ | 15¾ | 16½ | in |

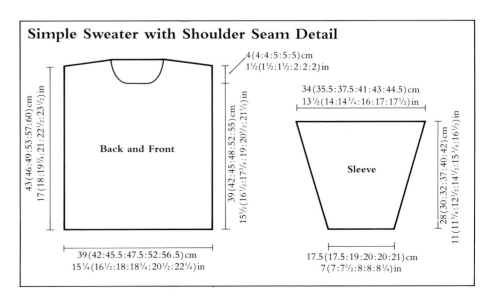

**Simple Sweater with Shoulder Seam Detail**

4(4:4:5:5:5)cm
1½(1½:1½:2:2:2)in

34(35.5:37.5:41:43:44.5)cm
13½(14:14¾:16:17:17½)in

Back and Front

43(46:49:53:57:60)cm
17(18:19¼:21:22½:23½)in

39(42:45:48:52:55)cm
15½(16½:17¾:19:20½:21½)in

Sleeve

28(30:32:37:40:42)cm
11(11¾:12½:14½:15¾:16½)in

39(42:45.5:47.5:52:56.5)cm
15¼(16½:18:18¾:20½:22¼)in

17.5(17.5:19:20:20:21)cm
7(7:7½:8:8:8¼)in

## MATERIALS

2(3: 4: 5) 100g of Rowan Magpie Aran in Brown (A).
2(3: 3: 3) hanks of same in Cream (B).
1(2: 2: 2) hanks of same in Black (C).
Pair each of 4mm (No 8/US 6) and 4½mm (No 7/US 7) knitting needles.
35(40: 45: 50)cm/14(16: 18: 20)in long open ended zip fastner.

## TENSION

18 sts and 23 rows to 10cm/4in square over pattern on 4½mm (No 7/US 7) needles.

## ABBREVIATIONS

See page 42

## NOTES

Read charts from right to left on right side rows and from left to right on wrong side rows unless otherwise stated. When working in colour pattern, strand yarn not in use loosely across wrong side to keep fabric elastic. When working squirrel motifs, use separate small balls for each coloured area and twist yarns together on wrong side at joins to avoid holes.

## BACK

With 4mm (No 8/US 6) needles and A, cast on 74(82: 90: 102) sts.
**1st rib row (right side)** K2, [p2, k2] to end.
**2nd rib row** P2, [k2, p2] to end.
Rib 2 rows in C and 2 rows in A.
Change to 4 1/2mm (No 7/US 7) needles. Beg with a k row, cont in st st throughout, work 6(8: 10: 12) rows in A. Work 11 rows of chart 1. With A, work 9(13: 17: 21) rows. Change to B and work 1 row. Work 3 rows of chart 2. With B, work 3 rows.
**Next row** P3(6: 9: 14)B, reading chart from right to left (thus reversing motif), p 1st row of chart 3, p12(14: 16: 18)B, reading chart from left to right, p 1st row of chart 3, p3(6: 9: 14)B.
**Next row** K3(6: 9: 14)B, reading chart from right to left, k 2nd row of chart 3, k12(14: 16: 18)B, reding chart from left to right, k 2nd row of chart 3, k3(6: 9: 14)B.
Work a further 22 rows as set. With B, work 3 rows. Work 3rd row, then 2nd and 1st rows of chart 2. With B, work 1 row. With A, work 10(14: 18: 24) rows. Work 9 rows of chart 4. Cont in A only until Back measures 44(49: 54: 59)cm/17¼(19¼: 21¼: 23¼)in from beg, ending with a wrong side row.
**Shape Shoulders**
Cast off 13(14: 16: 18) sts at beg of next 2 rows and 13(15: 16: 19) sts at beg of foll 2 rows. Cast off rem 22(24: 26: 28) sts.

## POCKET LININGS (make 2)

With 4½mm (No 7/US 7) needles and A, cast on 20(20: 22: 22) sts. Beg with a k row, work 24(26: 28: 30) rows in st st. Leave these sts on a holder.

## LEFT FRONT

With 4mm (No 8/US 6) needles and A, cast on 37(41: 45: 49) sts.
**1st rib row (right side)** K2, [p2, k2] to last 3 sts, k3.
**2nd rib row** K3, p2, [k2, p2] to end.
★★ Using small separate ball of A for the 3 sts at front edge and twisting yarns together on wrong side at joins, work as follows: Rib 2 rows in C and 2 rows in A, inc 2 sts evenly across last row on 4th size only. 37 (41: 45: 51) sts.
Change to 4½mm (No 7/US 7) needles. Keeping the 3 sts at front edge in garter st (every row k) and A and remainder in st st throughout, cont as follows:
With A and beg with a k row, work 6(8: 10: 12) rows. Work 11 rows of chart 1. Cont in A only, work 2 rows. ★★
Next row K3, p7(9: 10: 13), k20(20: 22: 22), p7(9: 10: 13).
**Next row** K.
Rep last 2 rows once more.
**Next row** K3, p7(9: 10: 13), cast off knitwise next 20(20: 22: 22) sts, p to end.
**Place Pocket**
Next row K7(9: 10: 13), k across st of pocket

## MEASUREMENTS

| To fit age | 4 | 6 | 8 | 10 | years |
|---|---|---|---|---|---|
| Actual chest | 82 | 91 | 100 | 113 | cm |
| measurement | 32 | 36 | 39½ | 44½ | in |
| Length | 44 | 49 | 54 | 59 | cm |
| | 17¼ | 19¼ | 21¼ | 23¼ | in |
| Sleeve seam | 30 | 33 | 36 | 40 | cm |
| | 11¾ | 13 | 14 | 15¾ | in |

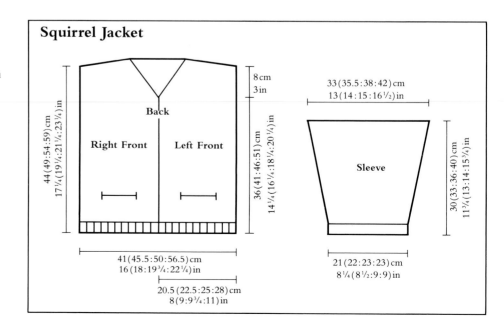

**Squirrel Jacket**

Back

Right Front    Left Front

44(49:54:59)cm
17¼(19¼:21¼:23¼)in

36(41:46:51)cm
14¼(16¼:18¼:20¼)in

8cm
3in

41(45.5:50:56.5)cm
16(18:19¾:22¼)in

20.5(22.5:25:28)cm
8(9:9¾:11)in

33(35.5:38:42)cm
13(14:15:16½)in

Sleeve

30(33:36:40)cm
11¾(13:14:15¾)in

21(22:23:23)cm
8¼(8½:9:9)in

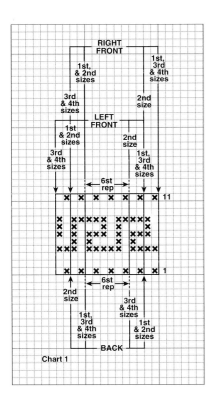

**Chart 1**

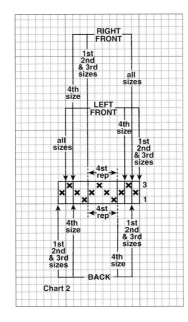

**Chart 2**

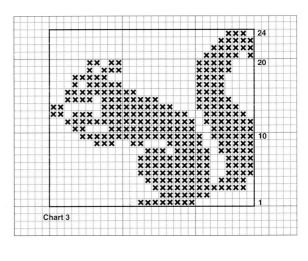

**Chart 3**

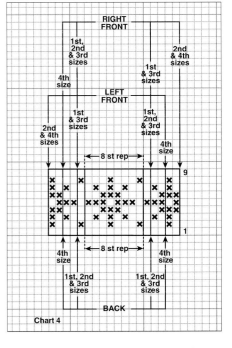

**Chart 4**

**KEY**

☐ Cream (B)

☒ Black (C )

lining, k to end.
Work 1(5: 9: 13) rows. Change to B and work 1 row. Work 3 rows of chart 2. With B, work 3 rows.

**Next row** K3A, p3(4: 6: 9)B, reading chart from left to right p 1st row of chart 3, p3(6: 8: 11)B.

**Next row** K3(6: 8: 11)B, reading chart from right to left, k 2nd row of chart 3, k3(4: 6: 9)B, 3A.
Work a further 22 rows as set. With B, work 3 rows. Work 3rd row, then 2nd and 1st rows of chart 2. With B, work 1 row. With A, work 10(14: 18: 24) rows. Work 4 rows of chart 4.

**Shape Neck**

**Next row** Patt to last 3 sts, turn; leave the 3 sts on a safety pin.
Keeping patt correct, dec one st at neck edge on next 4 rows. Cont in A only, dec one st at neck edge on every row until 26(29: 32: 37) sts rem. Cont straight until front matches Back to shoulder shaping, ending with a wrong side row.

**Shape Shoulder**

Cast off 13(14: 16: 18) sts at beg of next row. Work 1 row. Cast off rem 13(15: 16: 19) sts.

**RIGHT FRONT**

With 4mm (No 8/US 6) needles and A, cast on 37(41: 45: 49) sts.

**1st rib row (right side)** K5, [p2, k2] to end.
**2nd rib row** P2, [k2, p2] to last 3 sts, k3.
Work as given for Left Front from ★★ to ★★.
**Next row** P7(9: 10: 13), k20(20: 22: 22), p7(9: 10: 13), k3.
**Next row** K.
Rep last 2 rows once more.
**Next row** P7(9: 10: 13), cast off knitwise next 20(20: 22: 22) sts, p to last 3 sts, k3.

**Place Pocket**

**Next row** K10(12: 13: 16), k across sts of pocket lining, k to end.
Work 1(5: 9: 13) rows. Change to B and work 1 row. Work 3 rows of chart 2.

With B, work 3 rows.

**Next row** P3(6: 8: 11)B, reading chart from right to left, p 1st row of chart 3, p3(4: 6: 9)B, k3A.

**Next row** K3A, 3(4: 6: 9)B, reading chart from left to right, k 2nd row of chart 3, k3(6: 9: 11)B.
Complete to match Left Front, reversing shapings.

**LEFT SLEEVE**

With 4mm (No 8/US 6) needles and A, cast on 38(38: 42: 42) sts.
Work 2 rows in rib as given for Back. Rib 2 rows in C and 2 rows in A, inc 2 sts evenly across last row on 2nd size only. 38(40: 42: 42) sts.
Change to 4½mm (No 7/US 7) needles.
Beg with a k row, cont in st st, work 2 rows. Work 11 rows of chart 1 as indicated for Back, **at the same time**, inc one st at each end of 1st and 3 foll 3rd rows, working inc sts into patt. 46(48: 50: 50) sts. With A, work 9(13: 17: 21) rows, inc one st at each end of every 3rd row. 52(56: 60: 64) sts. With B, work 1 row. Work 3 rows of chart 2 as indicated for 4th size of Left Front. With B, work 3 rows, inc one st at each end of 1st row. 54(58: 62: 66) sts.

**Next row** P13(15: 17: 19), reading chart from left to right, p 1st row of chart 3, with B, p to end.

**Next row** Inc in first st, k12(14: 16: 18)B, reading chart from right to left, k 2nd row of chart 3, with B, k to last st, inc in last st. Work a further 22 rows as set, inc one st at each end of 2(2: 2: 4) foll 4th rows. 60(64: 68: 76) sts. With B, work 3 row. Work 3rd row, then 2nd and 1st rows of chart 2. With B, work 1 row. Cont in A only until Sleeve measures 30(33: 36: 40)cm/11¾(13: 14: 15¾)in from beg, ending with a wrong side row. Cast off.

**RIGHT SLEEVE**

Work as given for Left Sleeve, reversing squirrel motif by reading chart from left to right on right side rows and from right to left on wrong side rows.

**LEFT COLLAR**

With 4mm (No 8/US 6) needles, rejoin A at inside edge to 3 sts on left front safety pin. Work 12 rows in garter st, inc one st at inside edge on every 2nd row. Cont inc one st at inside edge as before, work 6 rows C, 6 rows A, 6 rows C, then cont in A only until there are 27 sts, ending at outside edge.

**Shape Collar**

**Next 2 rows** K14, yf, sl 1, yb, turn; sl 1, yb, k to end.
K4 rows. Rep last 6 rows until Collar fits up front neck to centre of back neck, ending at outside edge. Cast off.

**RIGHT COLLAR**

Work to match left collar.

**TO MAKE UP**

Join shoulder seams. Sew on sleeves, placing centre of sleeves to shoulder seams. Join side and sleeve seams. Sew on collar, then join back seam. Catch down pocket linings. Sew in zip fastner.

## MATERIALS

**Jacket** 6(7: 8) 50g hanks of Rowan DK Tweed.
Pair of 4mm (No 8/US 6) knitting needles.
Cable needle.
8 buttons.
**Beret** 2 50g hanks of Rowan DK Tweed.
Pair of 4mm (No 8/US 6) knitting needles.
Cable needle.

## MEASUREMENTS

| JACKET | | | | |
|---|---|---|---|---|
| To fit age | 2-3 | 3-5 | 5-7 | years |
| Actual chest | 72 | 80 | 90 | cm |
| measurement | 28½ | 31½ | 35½ | in |
| Length | 39 | 43 | 48 | cm |
| | 15½ | 17 | 19 | in |
| Sleeve seam | 25 | 28 | 33 | cm |
| | 10 | 11 | 13 | in |

| BERET | | | | |
|---|---|---|---|---|
| To fit average childs head. | | | | |

## TENSION

25 sts and 34 rows to 10cm/4in square over pattern on 4mm (No 8/US 6) needles.

## ABBREVIATIONS

**C6F** = sl next 3 sts onto cable needle and leave at front of work, k3, then k3 from cable needle;
**C4F** = sl next 2 sts onto cable needle and leave at front of work, k2, then k2 from cable needle.
Also see page 42.

## JACKET

### BACK

With 4mm (No 8/US 6) needles cast on 89(97: 111) sts.
**1st row (right side)** P1, [k1, p1] 1(3: 1) times, k6, ★ p1, [k1, p1] twice, k6; rep from ★ to last 3(7: 3) sts, p1, [k1, p1] 1(3: 1) times.
**2nd row** [P1, k1] 1(3: 1) times, p8, ★k1, p1, k1, p8; rep from ★ to last 2(6: 2) sts, [k1, p1] 1(3: 1) times.
**3rd row and 4th rows** As 1st and 2nd rows.
**5th row** P1, [k1, p1] 1(3: 1) times, C6F, ★p1, [k1, p1] twice, C6F; rep from ★ to last 3(7: 3) sts, p1, [k1, p1] 1(3: 1) times.
**6th row** As 2nd row.
**7th and 8th rows** As 1st and 2nd rows.
These 8 rows form patt. Cont in patt until Back measures 19(21: 24)cm/7½(8¼: 9½)in from beg, ending with a wrong side row.
**Shape Armholes**
Cast off 8(5: 8) sts at beg of next 2 rows. 73(87: 95) sts. Cont straight until Back measures 36(40: 45)cm/14¼(15¾: 17¾)in from beg, ending with a wrong side row.
**Shape Shoulders**
Cast off 10(12: 14) sts at beg of next 2 rows and 10(13: 14) sts at beg of foll 2 rows. Cast off rem 33(37: 39) sts.

### LEFT FRONT

With 4mm (No 8/US 6) needles, cast on 30(34: 41) sts.
**1st row (right side)** P1, [k1, p1] 1(3: 1) times, ★ k6, p1, [k1, p1] twice; rep from ★ to last 5 sts, k5.
**2nd row** Cast on 2, p8, ★ k1, p1, k1, p8; rep from ★ to last 2(6: 2) sts, [k1, p1] 1(3: 1) times.
**3rd row** P1, [k1, p1] 1(3: 1) times, k6, ★p1, [k1, p1] twice, k6; rep from ★ to last st, p1, k1 in last st.
**4th row** Cast on 2, k1, p1, k1, p8, ★k1, p1, k1, p8; rep from ★ to last 2(6: 2) sts, [k1, p1] 1(3: 1) times.
**5th row** P1, [k1, p1] 1(3: 1) times, C6F, ★ p1, [k1, p1] twice, C6F; rep from ★ to last 4 sts, p1, k1, p1, then k1, p1 in last st.
**6th row** Cast on 2, p3, k1, p1, k1, p8, ★k1, p1, k1, p8; rep from ★ to last 2(6: 2) sts, [k1, p1] 1(3: 1) times.
**7th row** P1, [k1, p1] 1(3: 1) times, ★ k6, p1, [k1, p1] twice; rep from ★ to last 2 sts, k1, k twice in last st.
**8th row** P twice in first st, p3, ★k1, p1, k1, p8; rep from ★ to last 2(6: 2) sts, [k1, p1] 1(3: 1) times.
These 8 rows set patt. Cont in patt as set, inc one st at end of next row and at same edge on foll 2 rows. 43(47: 54) sts. Work straight until Front matches Back to armhole shaping, ending with a wrong side row.
**Shape Armhole and Neck**
Cast off 8(5: 8) sts at beg of next row. Keeping armhole edge straight and patt correct, dec one st at neck edge on 2nd row and every foll 3rd row until 20(25: 28) sts rem. Cont straight until Front matches Back to shoulder shaping, ending with a wrong side row.

### Shape Shoulder
Cast off 10(12: 14) sts at beg of next row.
Patt 1 row. Cast off rem 10(13: 14) sts.

### RIGHT FRONT

With 4mm (No 8/US 6) needles cast on 30(34: 41) sts.
**1st row (right side)** K5, ★p1, [k1, p1] twice, k6; rep from ★ to last 3(7: 3) sts, p1, [k1, p1] 1(3: 1) times.
**2nd row** [P1, k1] 1(3: 1) times, ★p8, k1, p1, k1; rep from ★ to last 6 sts, p5, p twice in last st.
**3rd row** Cast on 2, k1, p1, k6, ★p1, [k1, p1] twice, k6; rep from ★ to last 3(7: 3) sts, p1, [k1, p1] 1(3: 1) times.
**4th row** [P1, k1] 1(3: 1) times, p8, ★k1, p1, k1, p8; rep from ★ to last st, k1, p1 in last st.
**5th row** Cast on 2, ★p1, [k1, p1] twice, C6F; rep from ★ to last 3(7: 3) sts, p1, [k1, p1] 1(3: 1) times.
**6th row** [P1, k1] 1(3: 1) times, ★p8, k1, p1, k1; rep from ★ to last st, p twice in last st.
**7th row** Cast on 2, k3, ★ p1, [k1, p1] twice, k6; rep from ★ to last 3(7: 3) sts, p1, [k1, p1] 1(3: 1) times.
**8th row** [P1, k1] 1(3: 1) times, ★p8, k1, p1, k1; rep from ★ to last 4 sts, p3, p twice in last st.
These 8 rows set patt. Complete to match Left Front, reversing shapings.

### SLEEVES

With 4mm (No 8/US 6) needles cast on 42(46: 50) sts.
**1st row (right side)** K2(4: 6), p1, [k1, p1] twice, ★k6, p1, [k1, p1] twice; rep from ★ to last 2(4: 6) sts, k to end.
**2nd row** P3(5: 7), k1, p1, k1, ★p8, k1, p1, k1; rep from ★ to last 3(5: 7) sts, p to end.
These 2 rows set patt. Cont in patt, inc one st at each end of 3rd row and 5 foll alt rows, then on every foll 4th row until there are 82(90: 100) sts, working inc sts into patt. Cont straight untul Sleeve measures 25(27: 33)cm/10(10½: 13)in from beg, ending with a wrong side row. Cast off.

### BACK WELT

With 4mm (No 8/US 6) needles cast on 7 sts.
**1st row** K1, [p1, k1] to end.
This row forms moss st patt. Cont in moss st until band, when slightly stretched, fits along lower edge of Back. Cast off.

### LEFT FRONT WELT, BUTTON BAND AND COLLAR

Join shoulder seams.
With 4mm (No 8/US 6) needles cast on 7 sts.
Work in moss st as given for Back Welt, until band fits along cast on edge off Left Front, easing band round lower shaped edge and up straight edge to beg of neck shaping.
**Shape Collar**
Cont in moss st, inc one st at beg of next row and at same edge on every foll 3rd row until there are 21 sts. Work straight until shaped edge of Collar fits up front neck to

shoulder, ending at straight edge.
**Next 2 rows** Moss st 14, sl 1, yf, turn, sl 1, moss st to end.
Moss st 4 rows. Rep last 6 rows until shaped edge of Collar fits up front neck to centre of back neck. Cast off.
Sew welt, band and collar in place.
Mark band along straight edge to indicate position of 4 buttons: first one 1cm/¼in above lower edge shaping, last one 1cm/¼in below beg of collar shaping and rem 2 evenly spaced between.

## RIGHT FRONT WELT, BUTTONHOLE BAND AND COLLAR
Work as given for Left Front Welt, Button Band and Collar, making buttonholes at markers as follows:
**Buttonhole row** Moss st 2, cast off 3, moss st to end.
**Next row** Moss st 2, cast on 3, moss st 2.

## SLEEVE CUFFS (make 2)
Work as given for Back welt until band fits along lower edge of Sleeve. Cast off.

## SIDE BELTS (make 2)
With 4mm (No 8/US 6) needles cast on 7 sts.
Work in moss st as given for Back Welt for 9cm/3½in. Dec one st at each end of next 2 rows. Work 3 tog and fasten off.

## TO MAKE UP
Join back seam of collar. Sew on back welt and sleeve cuffs. Sew on sleeves, placing centre of sleeves to shoulder seams and sewing last 3(2: 3)cm/1¼(¾: 1¼)in of sleeve tops to cast off sts at armholes. Join side and sleeve seams. Place side belts at sides and secure each end of belt in position with button. Sew on buttons.

## BERET
With 4mm (No 8/US 6) needles cast on 73 sts.
**1st row** K1, [p1, k1] to end.
This row forms moss st. Moss st 6 rows.
Inc row Inc in first st, moss st 3, ★ [m1, moss st 1] 3 times, moss st 2, work 3 times in next st, moss st 3; rep from ★ to last 6 sts, [m1, moss st 1] 3 times, moss st 2, work twice in last st. 113 sts.
**1st row (right side)** [Moss st 4, k6, moss st 4] to last st, moss st 1.
**2nd row** Moss st 1, [moss st 4, p6, moss st 4] to end.
**3rd (inc) row** [Moss st 4, m1, k6, m1, moss st 4] to last st, moss st 1.
**4th row** Moss st 1, [moss st 5, p6, moss st 5] to end.
**5th (inc) row** [Moss st 5, m1, C6F, m1, moss st 5] to last st, moss st 1.
**6th row** Moss st 1, [moss st 6, p6, moss st 6] to end.
**7th (inc) row** [Moss st 6, m1, k6, m1, moss st 6] to last st, moss st 1.
**8th row** Moss st 1, [moss st 7, p6, moss st 7] to end.
These 8 rows set patt.
**Inc row** [Patt 7, m1, patt 6, m1, patt 7] to last st, patt 1.
Patt 3 rows straight.
**Inc row** [Patt 8, m1, patt 6, m1, patt 8] to last st, patt 1.
Patt 3 rows straight.
**Inc row** [Patt 9, m1, patt 6, m1, patt 9] to last st, patt 1. 209 sts.
Patt 9 rows straight.
**Dec row** [Patt 8, work 2 tog, patt 6, work 2 tog tbl, patt 8] to last st, patt 1.
Patt 3 rows straight.
**Dec row** [Patt 7, work 2 tog, patt 6, work 2 tog tbl, patt 7] to last st, patt 1.
Patt 3 rows straight.
**Dec row** [Patt 6, work 2 tog, patt 6, work 2 tog tbl, patt 6] to last st, patt 1.
Cont in this way, dec 16 as set on every foll 4th row until 97 sts rem. Patt 3 rows straight.
**Dec row** [Patt 3, k2 tog, k2, k2 tog tbl, patt 3] to last st, patt 1.

**Next row** Patt 1, [patt 3, p4, patt 3] to end.
**Next row** [Patt 3, C4F, patt 3] to last st, patt 1.
**Next row** Patt 1, [patt 3, p4, patt 3] to end.
**Dec row** [Patt 1, work 2 tog, k4, work 2 tog tbl, patt 1] to last st, patt 1.
**Next row** Patt 1, [patt 2, p4, patt 2] to end.
**Next row** [Patt 2, C4F, patt 2] to last st, patt 1.
**Next row** Patt 1, [patt 2, p4, patt 2] to end.
**Dec row** [Work 2 tog, k4, work 2 tog tbl] to last st, patt 1.
**Next row** Patt 1, [patt 1, p4, patt 1] to end.
**Dec row** Patt 1, [C4F, p2 tog] to end.
P 1 row.
**Dec row** P1, [k2 tog, k2 tog tbl, p1] to end.
**Dec row** P1, [p2 tog] to end.
Break off yarn, thread end through rem 13 sts, pull up and secure. Join seam.

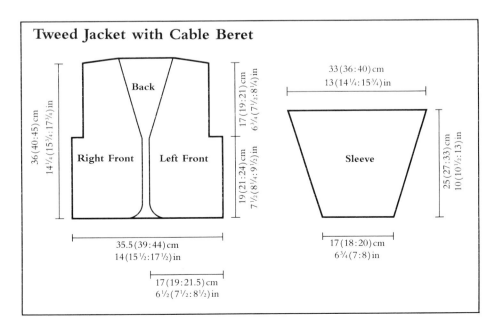

**Tweed Jacket with Cable Beret**

Back

Right Front    Left Front

36(40:45)cm
14¼(15¾:17¾)in

17(19:21)cm
6¾(7½:8¼)in

19(21:24)cm
7½(8¼:9½)in

35.5(39:44)cm
14(15½:17½)in

17(19:21.5)cm
6½(7½:8½)in

33(36:40)cm
13(14¼:15¾)in

Sleeve

25(27:33)cm
10(10½:13)in

17(18:20)cm
6¾(7:8)in

# Black and White Fair Isle Cardigan page 40

## MATERIALS

6(7: 8) 50g balls of Rowan DK
Handknit Cotton in Black (A).
5(5: 6) balls of same in Cream.
1 ball of same in Flame (B).
Pair each of 3¼mm (No 10/US 3) and
4mm (No 8/US 6) knitting
needles.
One each of 3¼mm (No 10/US 3) and
4mm (No 8/US 6) circular knitting
needles.
5 buttons.

## MEASUREMENTS

| To fit age | 4-6 | 6-8 | 8-10 years | |
|---|---|---|---|---|
| Actual chest | 89 | 100 | 111 | cm |
| measurement | 35 | 39½ | 43½ | in |
| Length | 41 | 46 | 51 | cm |
| | 16 | 18 | 20 | in |
| Sleeve seam | 31 | 34 | 38 | cm |
| | 12¼ | 13½ | 15 | in |

## TENSION

22 sts and 25 rows to 10cm/4in square
over pattern on 4mm (No 8/US 6)
needles.

## ABBREVIATIONS

See page 42.

## NOTES

Read chart from righ to left on right
side (k) rows and from left to right on
wrong side (p) rows. When working in
pattern strand yarn not in use loosely
across wrong side to keep fabric elastic.

## BACK AND FRONTS

Worked in one piece to armholes.
With 3¼mm (No 10/US 3) circular needle
and B, cast on 200(224: 248) sts. Work forwards and backwards in rows. K 1 row.
**Next row** Cast off purlwise 4 sts, p to
last 4 sts, cast off purlwise last 4 sts.
192(216: 240) sts.
Change to A.
**1st rib row (right side)** K3, [p2, k2] to
last 5 sts, p2, k3.
**2nd rib row** P3, [k2, p2] to last 5 sts, k2, p3.
Rep last 2 rows 3 times more, inc one st at
centre of last row. 193(217: 241) sts.
Change to 4mm (No 8/US 6) circular
needle.
Beg with a k row, work in st st and patt
from chart until work measures 25(28:
31)cm/9¾(11: 12¼)in from beg, ending
with a wrong side row.
**Right Front**
**Next row** Patt 48(54: 60), turn.
Work on this set of sts only until work
measures 28(31: 34)cm/11(12¼: 13½)in
from beg, ending with a wrong side row.
**Shape Neck**
Keeping patt correct, dec one st at neck
edge on next 5 rows then on every foll alt
row until 32(35: 38) sts rem. Cont straight
until work measures 41(46: 51)cm/16(18:
20)in from beg, ending with a right
side row.

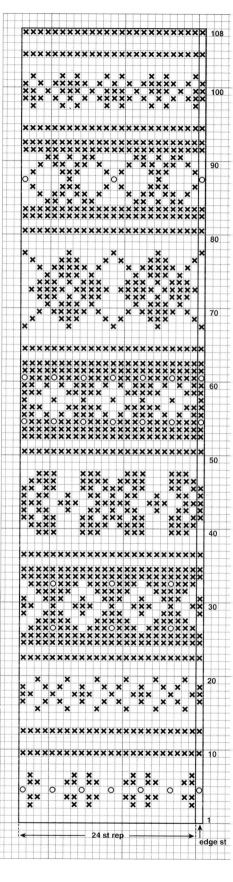

24 st rep

edge st

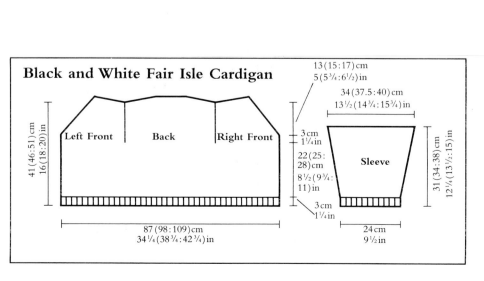

**KEY**

| | |
|---|---|
| ☐ | Black (A) |
| ☒ | Cream |
| ⊙ | Flame |

**Shape Shoulder**
Cast off 16(17: 19) sts at beg of next row.
Work 1 row. Cast off rem 16(18: 19) sts.
**Back**
With right side facing, rejoin yarn to rem sts and patt 97(109: 121) sts, turn. Work on this set of sts only until work measures 41(46: 51)cm/16(18: 20)in from beg, ending with a wrong side row.
**Shape Shoulders**
Cast off 16(17: 19) sts at beg of next 2 rows and 16(18: 19) sts at beg of foll 2 rows.
Leave rem 33(39: 45) sts on a holder.
**Left Front**
With right side facing, rejoin yarn to rem sts and patt to end. Complete to match Right Front, but ending with a wrong side row before shaping shoulder.

**SLEEVES**
With 3¼mm (No 10/US 3) needles and B, cast on 50 sts. K 1 row and p 1 row.
Change to A.
**1st rib row (right side)** K2, [p2, k2] to end.

**2nd rib row** P2, [k2, p2] to end.
Rep last 2 rows 3 times more, inc 3 sts evenly across last row. 53 sts.
Change to 4mm (No 8/US 6) needles.
**Next row** K last 3 sts of the 24 st patt rep, k the 24 sts twice, then k first 2 sts.
**Next row** P last 2 sts of the 24 st patt rep, p the 24 sts twice, then p first 3 sts.
Cont working from chart as set, at the same time, inc one st at each end of 3rd row, then on every foll 5th(4th: 4th) row until there are 75(83: 89) sts, working inc sts into patt.
Cont straight until Sleeve mesures 31(34: 38)cm/12¼(13½: 15)in from beg, ending with a wrong side row. Cast off.

**FRONT BAND**
Join shoulder seams.
With 3¼mm (No 10/US 3) circular needle, A and right side facing, k up 56(60: 64) sts along straight right front edge omitting the 2 rows of B at lower edge, 39(42: 45) sts along shaped edge to shoulder, k back neck sts, dec one st at centre, k up 39(42: 45) sts down

shaped edge of left front to beg of neck shaping and 56(60: 64) sts along straight edge omitting the 2 rows of B at lower edge. 222(242: 262) sts. Work backwards and forwards in rows. Beg with a 2nd row, work 2 rows in rib as given for Sleeves.
**Buttonhole row** Rib to last 50(54: 58) sts, [cast off 2, rib 8(9: 10) sts more] 4 times, cast off 2, rib to end.
**Next row** Rib to end, casting on 2 sts over those cast off in previous row.
Rib 1 row. Sew the cast off sts at each end of lower edge to row ends of band. Change to B.
**Next row** Pick up 2 sts from lower edge, k to end, then pick up 2 sts from lower edge. P 1 row. Cast off with B.

**TO MAKE UP**
Sew in sleeves, placing centre of sleeves to shoulder seams. Join sleeve seams. Sew on buttons.

---

# Simple Striped Sweater page 41

**BACK**
With 4mm (No 8/US 6) needles and C, cast on 78(84: 90: 98: 106) sts.
Beg with a k row, work in st st and stripe patt of 2 rows C, 2 rows B, 4 rows A, 2 rows B, 2 rows A, 2 rows B, 4 rows A and 2 rows B throughout until Back measures 39(42: 46: 51: 56)cm/15¼ (16½: 18: 20: 22)in from beg, ending with a wrong side row.

**Shape Shoulders**
Cast off 12(13: 14: 15: 17) sts at beg of next 2 rows and 12(13: 14: 16: 17) sts at beg of foll 2 rows. Leave rem 30(32: 34: 36: 38) sts on a holder.

**FRONT**
Work as given for Back until Front measures 35(37: 40: 45: 49)cm/13¾(14½: 15¾: 17¾:

## MEASUREMENTS

| To fit age | 2-3 | 3-4 | 4-6 | 6-8 | 8-10 | years |
|---|---|---|---|---|---|---|
| Actual chest | 78 | 84 | 90 | 98 | 106 | cm |
| measurement | 31 | 33 | 35½ | 38½ | 41½ | in |
| Length | 39 | 42 | 46 | 51 | 56 | cm |
| | 15¼ | 16½ | 18 | 20 | 22 | in |
| Sleeve seam | 25 | 28 | 34 | 38 | 40 | cm |
| | 10 | 11 | 13½ | 15 | 15¾ | in |

**MATERIALS**
4(4: 5: 7: 8) 50g balls of Rowan DK Handknit Cotton in Black (A).
3(3: 4: 6: 7) balls of same in Cream (B).
1(2: 2: 2: 3) balls of same in Flame (C).
Pair each of 3¼mm (No 10/US 3) and 4mm (No 8/US 6) knitting needles.

**TENSION**
20 sts and 28 rows to 10cm/4in square over st st on 4mm (No 8/US 6) needles.

**ABBREVIATIONS**
See page 42.

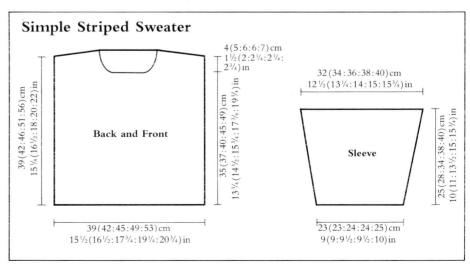

**Simple Striped Sweater**

Back and Front

39(42:46:51:56)cm
15¼(16½:18:20:22)in

35(37:40:45:49)cm
13¾(14½:15¾:17¾:19¼)in

4(5:6:6:7)cm
1½(2:2¼:2¼:
2¾)in

39(42:45:49:53)cm
15½(16½:17¾:19¼:20¾)in

Sleeve

32(34:36:38:40)cm
12½(13¼:14:15:15¾)in

25(28:34:38:40)cm
10(11:13½:15:15¾)in

23(23:24:24:25)cm
9(9:9½:9½:10)in

19¼)in from beg, ending with a wrong side row.

**Shape Neck**

**Next row** K31(33: 35: 38: 41), turn.
Work on this set of sts only. Dec one st at neck edge on every row until 24(26: 28: 31: 34) sts rem. Cont straight until Front matches Back to shoulder shaping, ending at side edge.

**Shape Shoulder**

Cast off 12(13: 14: 15: 17) sts at beg of next row. Work 1 row. Cast off rem 12(13: 14: 16: 17) sts.
With right side facing, slip centre 16(18: 20: 22: 24) sts onto a holder, rejoin yarn to rem sts and k to end. Complete to match first side.

**SLEEVES**

With 4mm (No 8/US 6) needles and C, cast on 46(46: 48: 48: 50) sts.
Beg with a k row, work in st st and stripe patt as given for Back, **at the same time**, inc one st at each end of 5th row and every foll 6th(6th: 7th: 7th: 6th) row until there are 64(68: 72: 76: 80) sts. Cont straight until Sleeve measures 25(28: 34: 38: 40)cm/10(11: 13 1/2: 15: 15¾)in from beg, ending with a wrong side row. Cast off.

**NECKBAND**

Join right shoulder seam.
With 3¼mm (No 10/US 3) needles, A and right side facing, pick up and k12(14: 16: 16: 18) sts down left front neck, k centre front sts, pick up and k12(14: 16: 16: 18) sts up right front neck, k back neck sts. 70(78: 86: 90: 98) sts. Beg with a p row, work in st st and stripe patt of 3 rows A, 2 rows B and 2 rows C. With C, cast off loosely.

**TO MAKE UP**

Join left shoulder and neckband seam, reversing seam on last 4 rows of neckband. Sew on sleeves, placing centre of sleeves to shoulder seams. Join side and sleeve seams, reversing seams on first and last 4 rows.

## Author's Acknowledgements

I would like to thank the following knitters for their invaluable help: Pat Church, Tina Egleton, Penny Hill, Maisie Lawrence, Frances Wallace.
I am particularly grateful to Tina Egleton for her great skill and dedication in checking the patterns, and to Sandra Lousada, not only for the beautiful photography but for her commitment to the project. I would like to thank Marie Willey for her lovely styling and Alison Walsh for her help on the shoot.
Thank you also to Heather Jeeves, my wonderful agent, and to Cindy Richards at Collins & Brown for creating the opportunity to work on this project.
Last, but not least, a special thank you to all the children and their parents:
Ashley, Amy, Anna, Ava, Billy, Callum, Connie, Eleanor, Hannah, Caitie, Kiyomi, Lily, Leina, Sharleyne, Ollie, Omar, Mickey, Joe, Mica and Yasmin.
Clothes provided by Nipper.

## Stockists/Distributors

Some of the designs in this book are available as kits. Write to Debbie Bliss at 9 Folkstone Road, Walthamstow, London E17 9SD for details.

For overseas stockists and mail-order information please contact:

**Australia** MacEwen Enterprises, 1/178 Cherry Lane, Laverton North, Vic 3026. Tel: 03 9369 3988.

**Belgium** Hedera, Pleinstraat 68, 3001 Leuven. Tel: (016) 232189

**Canada** Diamond Yarns, 9697 St Laurent, Montreal, Que H3L 2N1. Tel: 514 388 6188.

**Denmark** Filcolana A/S, Hagemannsvej 26-28, Box 151, 8600 Silkeborg. Tel: 86 81 02 11.

**France** Elle Tricote, 52 Rue Principale, 67300 Schiltigheim. Tel: 388 62 65 31.

**Germany** Wolle & Design, Wolfshovener Strasse 76, 52428 Julich-Stetternich. Tel: 02461/54735.

**Holland** Henk & Henrietta Beukers, Dorpsstraat 9, NL-5327 AR Hurwenen. Tel: 0418 661764.

**Hong Kong** Cheer Wool Co, 4 Fenwick Street, Wan Chai. Tel: 25273901.

**Iceland** Storkurinn, Kjorgardi Laugavegi 59, ICE-101, Reykjavik. Tel: 551 82 58.

**Italy** La Compagnia Del Cotone, Via Mazzini 44, 1-10123 Torino. Tel: (011) 87 83 81.

**Japan** Diakeito Co Ltd, 2-3-11 Senba-Higashi, Minoh City, Osaka 562. Tel: 0727 27 6604.

**Lithuania** Vakrina's Firm, Vivulskio 7-202, LT-2600 Vilnius. Tel: 632801.

**New Zealand** MacEwen Enterprises Ltd, 24b Allright Place, Mt Wellington, Auckland. Tel: 09527 3241.

**Norway** Eureka, PO Box 357, N1401 Ski. Tel: 64 86 55 40.

**Sweden** Wincent Sveavagen 94, 11350 Stockholm. Tel: (08) 673 70 60.

**UK** Rowan Yarns, Green Mill Lane, Holmfirth, West Yorkshire, HD7 1RW. Tel: 01484 681881.

**USA** Westminster Fibers Inc, 5 Northern Boulevard, Amherst, New Hampshire 03031. Tel: (603) 886 5041/5043.